NOBODY SEES THESE NATIONS

HOW DARKNESS RULES THE MANY THROUGH THE FEW

BOOK FIVE IN THE ELEVEN-BOOK UNSEEN SERIES

PAUL RENFROE

PARADIGM LIGHTHOUSE

Published by Paradigm Lighthouse

Freeport, FL 32439

ParadigmLighthouse.com

ISBN: 979-8-9924788-0-8 print, 979-8-9924788-1-5 ebook

LIBRARY OF CONGRESS CONTROL NUMBER: 2025901282

Published in the United States of America.

This book is dedicated to my loyal group of beta readers and paradigm underwriters. They have scrutinized and funded this Bible revelation ministry. Among them are Steve and Lundy Carpenter; may Lundy rest in peace with the Lord Jesus.

Check out the group Bible study discussion
of the unseen realm
on the companion
Podcast,
The Unseen Realm with Paul Renfroe and Friends

THE UNSEEN SERIES

Other Books by Paul Renfroe

WHAT PEOPLE ARE SAYING ABOUT THE UNSEEN SERIES...

This series of books has revelations in it that you won't find anywhere else. And these scripture revelations do a better job of explaining Bible mysteries than anything else I've heard. *Andrew Willis, Kentucky*

All glory be to God for giving Paul Renfroe the ability to not only perceive the unseen realm of spirits, both good and evil, but also to explain and teach others about this unseen reality. *Lisa Fulkerson, Ohio*

Solid evangelical Bible understanding are joined with the gifts of prophecy. I love how Paul bridges our gaps so our Bible study liberates us for a greater life in Jesus. *Paul Hughes, Kingdom Forerunners, Birmingham*

I find comfort and ease moving into 2025 with guidance from Paul Renfroe's books & podcast, as well as our local pastors and apostles. Having a spiritual family gives all of us faith that Jesus reigns in life, and—when we seek Him—in our own lives. *Holly G., Florida*

Starting in Genesis and onward, the *Unseen* Series simply guides each reader to see the unseen. Even those very familiar with the Scriptures will begin to see the clearer picture God has laid out for us in the Bible. You will begin to see things differently, beyond the surface, and into the unseen where God desires each of us to function as His children. These books will give much insight, but not only that, they will strengthen your vision of God's call on your life and enable you to "fight the good fight of faith." *Jeff Ellis, Wisconsin*

I would just say to any potential reader, through this book, you will know God better and experience a greater revelation of who He is. I have experienced so many WOW moments through these studies.

Thanks to Paul Renfroe's *Unseen* Series books and podcast, it's been my privilege to explore the supernatural realm. Even more, this series has taught me the great value of going deeper and deeper in God's Word. I've become more than a surface reader; now I'm searching out the meaning. The books have taught me how to truly receive revelation from the Bible.

Paul's life has been devoted to God's Word. His superior crafts-manship and intellect have helped me explore the spirit realm. The *Unseen* Series has truly opened my eyes to the unseen dimension. ***Barbara Johnson, Florida***

Paul's *Unseen* Series of books and podcast has opened my eyes to hidden Bible mysteries. I've learned how to study scripture in new ways. A common theme in the series is a meek attitude and an open mind. These help you gain more Biblical understanding, and God reveals new life principles, overlooked before. It is a rewarding experience to walk that path. I think you will really enjoy reading each book! ***Rebecca Porter, Texas***

Your books do reveal the Bible's reality of an unseen enemy, and people need to be aware! Hindrances in the spirit realm blind family members and keeps us apart. God is exposing some truth to set us free. From your writing, I see why they call you a story teller and explainer! ***Larry Brewer, Indiana***

Paul powerfully warns in this book not to be a cowardly believer in Jesus Christ, because we are in spiritual battles of the unseen world. He will shoot a challenging spiritual bullet across the bow of your mind, so you can take up your God-given authority in Jesus' name. ***David Goode, Kentucky***

Paul Renfroe combines the revealed and established words of God to build upwards upon Christ's foundation, drawing upon His buttresses of truth and wisdom, insight and knowledge. God is using Paul's obedience to the Spirit and Word to challenge centuries of limitations and reconcile the reality of seen and unseen realms. Paul's writings and his life are both testaments to the loving, revelatory, and unchanged nature of the Living God. I pray your eyes are opened by reading Paul's *Unseen* series of books, blogs, and podcasts—that you can delight in the Bible revelations of Jesus. Through Paul's writings, you really can live as a new, transformed creation. Jesus is calling, and you're not crazy for hearing. Get ready to grow. ***Katie R. Dale, Germany—advocate, artist, and author of award-winning* But Deliver Me from Crazy.**

In these days of uncertainty, it is more important than ever to understand the spiritual dynamics in operation in this world. These hidden powers impact our lives in ways we may not recognize. Ignorant of our enemy, we are likely duped by him.

Paul Renfroe is a brilliant scholar gifted to explain in everyday terms many complex, little known Bible truths which are often misunderstood. His writing is meticulously researched, then tested by beta readers prior to publication. The resulting trustworthiness and accuracy makes your time with his books worthwhile. They will equip you for victorious living and powerful function as a member of God's army. ***Linda Roeder. Ohio—Chairman of the Board,* Restoring the Foundations International, *and author of* Right Relationships.**

Paul Renfroe's *Unseen* Series remedied my older paradigms and shifted my understanding. Each book is a quick read—a page turner with a unique perspective on commonly held but incomplete perceptions. Whether or not you agree, Paul's outlook is intriguing and keeps your attention. He supports his interpretations with excellence, using many Bible citations that you see in a new way.

When we read the Bible, most of us conceive a picture or explanation instantly, and that paradigm sticks. From Apostle Paul's viper bite to the creation of everything, we envision what Scripture says, to feel comfortable with the message.

Reading Paul's books changed my picture of many things in the Bible. I found important words and phrases I had never noticed before. I have learned a lot about my Bible. There is something for everyone in the first five books of the *Unseen* Series. My dear friends and relatives have been thankful that I gave them one of Paul's educational and entertaining books. Five Stars! ***Gerald Mullis, Florida***

In our Christian walk, it is imperative to see God for who He really is. Otherwise, we misinterpret Him as well as ourselves, and fall into the devil's deception.

God is a spirit. When we follow Jesus, His perfect Holy Spirit lives in us and makes us each a perfect spirit. Redeeming us by the Blood, God restores His image in us. But if we fail to see God with the correct lenses, we totally miss Christ Jesus. Tragically, we lose our very identity, and the destiny He wrote for us. Our intended function never materializes.

We are spirits, born by faith in Jesus' death and resurrection. Although we live in a body, we operate in more than one dimension. Not knowing it does not change who we are, but exposes us to evil tricks, false beliefs, and deception. Religion is one way the enemies have deceived us.

The Bible says we are citizens of Heaven. God's plan is that we operate as He does. As a born-again, Holy-Spirit-filled Christian, you are a spirit, just as Jesus is, living in the spirit realm. God made us alive and seated us with Jesus in the spirit realm. We can rule and reign with Jesus now. The kingdom is here, in us and through us!

When we learn truly who God is, then we will know who we are. I've read the first three books in Paul Renfroe's *Unseen* Series. They directly confront and correct deceptions in the Body of Christ. Paul writes with tact and the Spirit of revelation.

I say to every reader that Jesus' promise is good. *Seek God's Kingdom and His Righteousness, and all these things will be added unto you.* The most valuable *things?* to know Him, to see yourself as He sees you, and to function as He intended—a spirit-ruler with Him. ***Grover Scott, Florida***

CONTENTS

INTRODUCTION

Where God is, is the most real world. People whom He claims form a nation filled with His joyful presence and love. In contrast, darkness snares Earth's nations into destruction, using a few bottlenecks and chokepoints to rule many people.

God's Word reveals He wants us in a partnership with Him. He is spirit, and we have a spirit's relationship directly with Him.

> But the hour is coming, and now is, when the true
> worshipers will worship the Father in spirit and
> truth; for the Father is seeking such to worship
> Him. God is Spirit, and those who worship Him
> must worship in spirit and truth. (John 4:23–24)

Also in the unseen realm are enemies. These spirits compete to damn every soul; by dominating Earth's nations, they strive for greatest efficiency. The fallen Lucifer uses his archangelic power only to advance himself.

For you [Lucifer] have said in your heart:

'I will ascend into heaven,
I will exalt my throne above the stars of God;
I will also sit on the mount of the congregation
On the farthest sides of the north;
I will ascend above the heights of the clouds,
I will be like the Most High. (Isaiah 14:13–14)

WHY KNOW THIS?

We love God, who revealed it for a reason: we are His military in that invisible contest. We must know the enemy He has appointed us to defeat.

On this rock I will build My church, and
the gates of Hades shall not prevail against it.
(Matthew 16:18)

Jesus describes gates which protect hell's possessions. The devil told Jesus that nations are his to dominate and distribute. But with our divine assignment to shrink Lucifer's territorial domination, we need increased function for the unseen in our time. Nobody knows the nations as the devil does, but our assignment requires us to.

Go therefore and make disciples of all the nations.
(Matthew 28:19)

IT'S YOUR CHOICE

You may fear that knowledge; many do. An old saying is, "this far, and no farther." Christians can cocoon in a self-centered spiritual comfort zone. We may feel the tug of heavenly realms, yet fear the spirit world, or even disdain those who seek effectiveness in it. I know that way of thinking because it was mine for a long time.

The choice is yours. You really can function as a spirit. It is what the Father wants for you. It's the purpose of the reconciling gospel and the filling Spirit.

The Paradigm Lighthouse ministry includes our books, blogs, and podcasts. Each equips you for more effectiveness in both seen and unseen; participants report new spiritual vitality. Being Christ-like includes the full activation of your spirit, with all its holy capabilities.

WHAT HAPPENED TO ME

Over fifty years following Jesus, I've had many experiences only possible for living human spirits but didn't know it for the first four decades.

In my nightly dreams were spirit beings, both holy and unholy. In waking visions I heard and saw spirit-beings and perceived the reality principles of the unseen. Specific knowledge would explode in my head about people and events which I could only know from God. Sometimes it was like reading the back of my eyelids.

I thank God He was leading my wife the same way, so that neither of us was totally alone. Many such experiences fired our curiosity.

THE UNUSUAL ONE

God has provided churches for our stability and growth; we respect their boundaries and submit to their authorities. But my wife and I quickly learned to keep our spiritual experiences between us, because few others could relate. The ministers in my circles offered little certainty about the spirit world of God; some sought to shame us. So we dove into the Word of God to seek explanations.

In many fellowships, there are unspoken limits on spiritual experiences, so you can feel unusual and isolated. I know because early in my leadership years, I disdained spiritual perception as uncontrollable. Hiding behind the skirts of the Bible's exclusive authority, I refused the very expectations that God promised in it. The Scripture's authority to reveal could not exceed my comfort zone, a mistake anyone can make.

It hurts to remember my closed response when friends shared their encounters with the unseen. When perception arose in me, I finally yielded, and regretted my closed-mindedness.

After a long isolation, my wife and I learned about the prophetic movement, and the network of churches and training centers such as Christian International. How relieved my wife and I were in 2006 to learn that we weren't the only ones.

Reader, you are not the only one either. One purpose of the *Unseen* Series of books, blogs, and podcast is a community of believers at ease with unseen experiences. After we gain the Bible's explanations, we both stimulate and comfort one another, as evidenced in our group discussion podcasts.

THE WORD HAS THE EXPLANATION

So, I urge you to do what I did. If what I was seeing, hearing, and feeling was from God, it would be in His Word somehow. It didn't matter if I had never seen it, nor my pastors or friends. Nobody knows everything, so I interrogated the Bible myself and unearth its paradigm of reality.

Our understanding of reality must always improve, and the Bible —God's inspired and trustworthy Word—is how. These pages cite many well-known Scriptures, for you to re-read. Don't skip the well-known ones as if you already understand them. I too read them hundreds of times before I saw the unseen through them. God's Word reveals, but not all at once. Re-reading and re-explaining is an essential ingredient of receiving what He put there for us.

In this book, I take God's words at face value within their context as our Lord did. Jesus saw His life in the Old Testament using interpretive patterns we can safely use.

THE DISCOVERIES AHEAD

My purposeful use of the word *discovery* is to convey an expectation: new Bible insights lay ahead for you in these pages. But they are not new truths, nor the low-hanging fruit we most often preach or study. Awaiting you are the mysteries that Apostle Paul often mentioned.

> However, we speak wisdom among those who are
> mature, yet not the wisdom of this age, nor of the
> rulers of this age, who are coming to nothing.
> But we speak the wisdom of God in a mystery,
> the hidden wisdom which God ordained before
> the ages for our glory, which none of the rulers of
> this age knew, ... (1 Corinthians 2:6–8a)

He names three families of wisdom. First is *the wisdom of this age:* our general knowledge, common sense, and habits. The second wisdom belongs to *the rulers of this age*, those unseen rulers who outlive people. Several chapters ahead review that wisdom.

But the third is God's secret wisdom. It predates the other two, His decisive decrees before the foundation of the world. Hidden for so long from all humanity and unseen enemies, the gospel now reveals it. The long wait was God's feint, seducing satan to orchestrate Jesus' crucifixion for sin.

> ....for had they known, they would not have crucified
> the Lord of glory. (2:8b)

Elsewhere in the *Unseen* Series

To study God's three overarching decrees, see chapter eight of the *Unseen* Series' third book, titled *Nobody Sees This Creation: The Origin of the Devil and His Replacements.*

WHAT YOU GAIN

You may want to know where these discoveries will lead, and how things will change for you. If that's you, start with chapter 17, *Not Against Flesh and Blood*. The subheadings there are:

- Be a Disciple
- Snapshot of Existence
- Understand Church History
- Understand Your Place
- Understand God's Word
- Loyalty Beyond Yourself
- You're in the Army Now
- Understand the Holy Spirit's Prayers
- Understand the Enemy
- Deliverance from Demons
- Penetrating People-Groups
- Interceding for Nations
- Discipleship, Evangelism, and Missions
- Represent the Judge
- Body Politic
- Now Start

To prepare you for these discoveries and their implementation, three basic Bible concepts will appear throughout.

1: THE UNSEEN REALM IS SPIRITS

Jesus taught Christians are born as spirits. Everyone's natural birth produced a unique soul and body. You weren't there before. Likewise, your faith-birth produced a unique individual. When you believed in Jesus Christ, you were born as a living human spirit that didn't exist previously.

Though very familiar, these verses about your spirit nature may have never been clear.

> Most assuredly, I say to you, unless one is born of
>   water and the Spirit, he cannot enter the
>   kingdom of God. That which is born of the flesh
>   is flesh, and that which is born of the Spirit is
>   spirit. Do not marvel that I said to you, 'You
>   must be born again.' The wind blows where it
>   wishes, and you hear the sound of it, but cannot
>   tell where it comes from and where it goes. So is
>   everyone who is born of the Spirit. (John 3:6–8)

Filled with the Spirit may be deep, yet filled is not all you are. Jesus described us as wind, perceptible yet unseen and unaccountable. His sentence includes you as a Christian: *So is everyone who is born of the Spirit.*

People who are dead in spirit know there's something distinctly real in us but can't put their finger on it. Disdaining to follow Jesus, they are not born again as spirit. Unbelievers are born only once, flesh and blood and soul, but no spirit.

Being born of the Spirit is not self-centered. Salvation is much more than mere religion or mental agreement. We are spirits aligned with God Almighty, THE Spirit. The primary reality is where God is.

We are born into a kingdom: God's. You and I act on His behalf in both the unseen and the visible, in the heavenly realms and on Earth. By faith in Jesus, you are born into an invisible world of spirits, and it's more present to you now than the visible world.

That's why full effectiveness requires you to see the unseen nations.

2: THE BATTLE FRONT IS NATIONS

The Bible is the written revelation of God and the spirit world. Nations, past and present, are the battle line of the two invisible kingdoms. The devil wants to control the most people with the fewest partners, and nations are his primary method ever since Babel's division.

Scripture's *nation* differs from ours. To us, it means a politically bound geographic area under a distinct government. This definition arose only in the last few centuries.

For most of history, *nation* meant people-groups. Language and culture identified them, rather than government or boundaries. Our word *ethnic* denotes these people-groups. It comes from the Bible's Greek word for nations, ἔθνος, transliterated *ethnos.*

Generational family lineage transmits common language; shared culture and religions result. Outsiders often named a place for its resident language group; even after the group migrated away, their name was synonymous with their original region.

Empires form the backbone of history. A people-group would integrate diverse language-groups under its government. Military force permitted such dominance, but economic and cultural habits, perceived as sources of power, encouraged submission.

Thus Alexander's sprawling empire imposed the Greek culture *(a.k.a.* Hellenism*)* upon many nations. It became the worldwide trade system because the culture remained even after his empire subsided.

Throughout this book, the word *nation* signifies a people-group. Such a nation may not live in one place or have a unique shared government or a political identity. They may be dominant or dominated.

Synonyms for Bible nations include *race, ethnicity, family, tribe, lineage, people, language* and *language-group.* I often use the word *ethnos* as a stand-in for nations.

The war in the heavenly realms drives the drama of nations on

Earth. Darkness wants to corrupt large numbers of people through their few leaders.

3: THE NATION ISRAEL

Finally, the Bible primarily concerns the people group, Israel. The political nation of Israel is often engaged in defense against surrounding nations. The entire history of that people-group has required war for survival.

How do Israel and its conflicts fit into the unseen kingdom contest? Hidden in the public animosity toward Israel is incitement by the powers of darkness. There, Israel is hated for one reason: God claimed them as His people-group.

The devil and his minions war against all whom God favors. Apostle Paul said the Body of Christ is now grafted into the one people-group God has claimed. As God's *ethnos*, the Church of Jews and Gentiles receives the animosity of darkness because hell's gates must retreat before us.

Every spirit in the unseen realms knows the ultimate destiny of the rebels. Apostle John wrote it in his vision.

> The devil has come down to you, having great wrath,
> because he knows that he has a short time. (Reve-
> lation 12:12)

PRODUCTION NOTES

Three protocols in this book may be different for you at first but their compelling rationale makes them easy for you to accommodate.

CAPITALIZATION

To identify participants in the unseen world, each book in the *Unseen* Series follows these capitalization guidelines.

In written English, capitalization suggests honor and esteem. The first letter is capitalized in all pronouns for God or a Person of the Trinity. Today's style guidelines call this archaic; I mean it respectfully. It also helps distinguish the many spirits in the unseen world.

I do not use an uppercase first letter for any personal being of darkness. The word *satan* means "accuser" in the Bible, describing his function. Like our words *boss* or *nurse,* such job names are not capitalized. Lucifer is satan's given name from God before rebelling (Isaiah 14), and has a first letter cap.

There are unseeable personal entities which are active, but the Bible reveals them in a shaded way, indirectly; they are implied, rather than stated. Names for these entities have an uppercase first letter, such as *Creation, Sin,* and *Earth.* When lowercase first letter, those words indicate the acts of creating and sinning, or refer to land, dirt, or acreage.

ALPHABETS

In the *Unseen* Series, I sometimes include New Testament words in their original Greek alphabet, so you can test my interpretation. If that does not interest you, proceed without hesitation; those words will also be transliterated into the English alphabet.

SYNONYMS

Only three parties dominate the following pages: God, darkness, and mankind. To prevent monotony, I use a wide variety of synonymous phrases.

For example, the phrase *"our first parents"* denotes Adam and Eve. *"The archangel"* in passages about Lucifer obviously refers to him.

People, human beings, humankind, mankind, and *mortal race* are all customary names for humanity. *Ethnos, nation,* and *people group* describe tribes and families of people.

I use two phrases that may be new. Humans are *image-creatures* because we're the only creatures ever made in God's image. Christians are *spirit-creatures* as the only race with living spirits in created mortal bodies. They are explained further in the *Unseen* Series' first installment.

PART ONE

LIFTING THE CURTAIN

Many 21st century Christians perceive the spirit world. One reason is the Church's lengthy maturity process. Another is necessity, because our unseen enemies are unveiling themselves. They seduce people to welcome their domination and penalize us who love Jesus Christ.

But in the Bible's four thousand years, increased perception occurs repeatedly. God often lifted the curtain between the seen and the unseen, like we experience today. In Part One, Babel and Abraham provide us two early examples, followed by Moses.

To perceive the unseen is a Christian's birthright. We are born in spirit and it's where spirits live, including God Himself.

But why do only a minority of Christians manifest this birthright? A paradigm that matches the Bible's paradigm is necessary.

CHAPTER 1

WHAT IS A PARADIGM?

A PARADIGM IS THE WAY WE PERCEIVE AND INTERPRET reality. Synonyms include *grid, outlook, worldview, template, lens, explanation, operating system*, and the like. These govern our minds and imagination by limiting what we consider possible.

Our explanation of reality defines what to fear and desire, and dictates how to evaluate people and events. When your life doesn't hold what the Bible promises, check your paradigm.

REVELATION IN IMPLICATIONS

The Bible reveals a supernatural world with words of the natural world. We can't see God, spirits, devils, sin, love, nations, or kingdoms. The key concepts of the Bible are all unseen. How can God reveal them in our words?

When we delve into scripture, we discover the reality it assumes. Its implications force modifications in our worldview. The Bible does not directly describe the unseen realm, nor nations' role in it, but indirectly. The world of the unseeable spirits is the assumed reality necessary for the truths it does state directly and explicitly.

The Standard of Explanatory Power is an important Bible study principle used throughout the *Unseen* Series. New worldviews must explain more than the previous one. To put it another way, the more explanation a passage requires, the weaker your paradigm.

Elsewhere in the *Unseen* Series

To identify those unstated truths requires the Bible study technique of reverse engineering, described in Book Two of the series, *Nobody Sees This Unseen Realm: How to Unlock Bible Mysteries.*

COMMON UNBIBLICAL PARADIGMS

To function effectively as a spirit, you must update your paradigm that you are a living spirit by being born again.

Church is the focal point of our Christian practices, and it's easy to think that our church is God's kingdom. However, Jesus used the word *church* only three times, compared to fifty times for the *kingdom of God* and thirty-two times for the *kingdom of heaven*. Whereas the church is organized with members, a kingdom is an organic citizenship under a king with enemies.

A common "operating system" is that church exists to support my Christian life and my happy relationship with God. With that assumption, *peace* means hassle-free living full of happiness. This is neither biblical nor historical, as martyrs past and present will testify. By using faith to feather our nests, by loving our comfort more than Him, we subject ourselves to more severe judgment.

Many avid Christians teach and counsel that we only need to know God, and He will deal with the devil. I know, because it was my churches' paradigm for decades. But if we truly know Him, we receive all of what He reveals, not just the comfortable parts. If we refuse, we are severely accountable.

Unbiblical paradigms are many; this is just a sampling of common ones. Using them, most Christians avoid knowledge about the kingdom of darkness. Such a cowardly policy excuses Christians from the kingdom standard of the Bible.

BRAVERY A CHRISTIAN REQUIREMENT

We are citizens of God's kingdom, ambassadors to the unsaved. God expects us to recognize His enemies effectively and represent His kingdom while rescuing people from them.

But to avoid intimidation by the devil, many Christians avoid knowing our enemies' habits, and thus cannot discern hostile deceptions. As the saying goes, *you can run, but you can't hide.* That's the mildest reality, because you can't outrun those evil spirits.

And to top it off, Judgment Day awaits us all. God excludes cowardly fearfulness from heaven and lumps such people with more obvious sinners in hell.

> He who overcomes shall inherit all things, and I will
> be his God and he shall be My son. But the
> cowardly, unbelieving, abominable, murderers,
> sexually immoral, sorcerers, idolaters, and all liars
> shall have their part in the lake which burns with
> fire and brimstone. (Revelation 21:7–8)

To be a Christian, *like Christ,* you must exhibit His awareness and bravery about the enemies of His kingdom by updating to the Bible paradigm and putting aside ignorance, no matter how distasteful to your comfort zone.

Apostle Paul was not ignorant, nor did he want us to be, *lest Satan should take advantage of us; for we are not ignorant of his devices* (2 Corinthians 2:11).

Flip it: if we *are* ignorant, then satan *will* take advantage of us with his schemes.

CHAPTER 2

THE BIBLE PARADIGM OF REALITY

GOD CREATED MANY SPIRITS BEFORE HE MADE US. THESE include the cherubim and angels who obey Him and serve those He favors. As a spirit, you are born by faith in Jesus Christ into the company of these holy spirits who serve Him faithfully, and everyone whom He favors—like you.

REALITY IS SPIRITS

Now that we are spirit, soul, and body, as Adam and Eve were, we are the image of God restored. That reproducing image is threatening enough to our unseen enemies, and then it got even worse for them.

God filled us with His Holy Spirit. That makes us more than our first parents were. Not only are we spirits, we are spirits with a Holy Spirit inside of us, intimate with us.

Several scriptures talk about these realities. When you see them together, you realize you are a spirit in a world of spirits.

> God is Spirit, and those who worship Him must
> worship in spirit and truth. (John 4:24)

If anyone loves Me, he will keep My word; and My
Father will love him, and We will come to him
and make Our home with him. (John 14:23)

Are they [angels] not all ministering spirits sent forth
to minister for those who will inherit salvation?
(Hebrews 1:14)

For we do not wrestle against flesh and blood, but
against principalities, against powers, against the
rulers of the darkness of this age, against spiritual
hosts of wickedness in the heavenly places. (Ephesians 6:12)

Thus, we speak of the *unseen*, the realm of all spirits—both holy
and unholy, both for God and against Him, both for you and against
you. As a Christian you are in it, born again as a spirit when you
yielded to Jesus.

REALITY IS SPIRITUAL WAR

Ephesians 6:12 above is Apostle Paul's oft-quoted teaching that Christians are at war with darkness. It's not a war to preserve our lifestyle from
hassle or devilish debacle, nor is it a war with people over our values.

In the biblical paradigm, we are living human spirits. As such, we
inhabit a world of spirits including both obedient ones and rebel
ones.

Any kingdom has adversaries, God's kingdom most of all. Not all
angels and cherubim remained loyal to God, and instead became a
kingdom of dark, unholy, rebel spirits, namely the fallen angels and
demons led by satan.

Lucifer is not the anti-god. He is not divine and never has been,
although he would like to think so. He is a created being, like we are.

God created him as an archangel of equal rank to Michael and Gabriel. Forfeiting the rank did not erase his angelic nature.

The fallen Lucifer, become satan, is not omnipresent, does not know everything, and cannot interact with more than one person at a time. His kingdom requires partners, and he uses a system of iron-grip delegation.

We Christians love and worship God. When we fail to, we confess and repent. But satan and the angels he led in rebellion cannot repent. They have the fires of God's wrath within them and a craving for moisture to relieve it.

Their delusions and hatred are a last gasp against God's mortal race. For satan and his partners, people are only cannon fodder in their war against God. But you, they now recognize, because now you are a spirit, like they are.

You are far more threatening to them than you yet know. They aim their self-defense at us. The *Unseen* Series identifies satan's most persistent strategies to corrupt his replacements and shows the biblical response to them.

PARADIGM COUNTERFEITING

Christians are not the only ones with exposure to the unseen world. Throughout human history, there has been access to spirits apart from God and His revelation. False religions, idolatry, witchcraft, sorcery, and other evils all have a grip because they work. By these practices, people can have a form of spiritual function without the true God.

Certainly, we Christians must not follow such practices, nor do we fellowship blindly with someone merely because they like the unseen realm or deal with spirits. Apostle John gave clear guidance.

> Beloved, do not believe every spirit, but test the spir-
> its, whether they are of God. (1 John 4:1)

For this Bible injunction to make sense, two assumptions must be true. First, we definitely encounter spirits, both holy and unholy. Second, we can become proficient in testing spirits. When ministries and Christians ignore spirits or cower in fear, that proficiency is immature.

Apostle Paul's war description above assumes the same readiness and capabilities that Apostle John did:

- you and I do encounter spirits;
- we can recognize them; and
- we can distinguish holy ones from unholy, and true from counterfeit.

It's not flesh and blood such as witches whom we wrestle but their unseen backers. The spirits of evil literally use people to death. Only our kingdom offers rescue from being sucked dry by satan's dominion.

PARADIGM OF NATION-CLAIMING

In these pages, we explain the biblical paradigm of people-groups, and why the ruling spirits of the unseen realm claim nations. To snare as many people as possible, darkness uses a few with bribes, who then lead many people into willful hostility to God. These few act as bottle-necks and chokepoints for the entire *ethnos*. Darkness seeks to ruin the many through the few; God seeks to bless the many through the few.

Jesus gave us a mandate before He ascended into heaven.

Go therefore and make disciples of all the nations.
(Matthew 28:19)

The rise of political nations and global travel has channeled this mandate into missionary service. But the *ethnos* concept is what Jesus was referring to: *make disciples of every people-group.* Luke's record of the similar admonition names the first three to target in their execution of His command.

> You shall be witnesses to Me in Jerusalem, and in all
> Judea and Samaria, and to the end of the earth.
> (Acts 1:8)

With this comes a new understanding of nations and how we fit in, the central focus of this book.

PARADIGM BENEFITS

If your paradigm matures, your faith strengthens from better alignment with the Bible's implied reality. With a more biblical grid, you fit better. In both seen and unseen, you have a new effectiveness from an accurate and powerful perception of reality.

Nations are under dark dominion. Spirits influence large numbers through the few. Our enemy in the spiritual war uses choke-points of the few to control the many. Wrestling them requires this biblical knowledge about *ethnos.*

You can forgive their pawns and have mercy for their victims. Evangelism gains new vitality; you are rescuing new believers to God's army, for the unseen competition.

This outlook activates your godly influence at a higher level. You will have weightier Bible authority in your neighborhood, politics, citizenship, or civic engagement. The paradigm of nations revolutionizes our understanding of Israel and America, our reading of both Old and New Testament, our church engagement, and our walk with God.

It explains the entire flow of the Bible's history in a usable way. You occupy two societies, visible and invisible. This paradigm unleashes your effectiveness to represent God's kingdom in both.

NEW RULERS

God created the unseen first, then the visible. But when He cast Lucifer and the rebel angels down to Earth, they ruined the original creation into dark and formless void of deep water.

Five Bible passages explained the origin of the devil and why he is on Earth, in Book Three, *Nobody Sees This Creation: The Origin of the Devil and His Replacements.*

God's six-day, staccato terror assault upon the ruinous rebels re-formed and re-filled the Earth. Day Six punctuated the divine assault on darkness with the first creatures ever in His image: people.

He mandated our first parents to multiply and fill rule the Earth, making people the replacements of Earth's previous dominators. The nations that people form are a central element in that contest.

SATAN'S EARLY STRATEGIES

Book Four outlined satan's first four strategies against God's image-creatures. Its title: *Nobody Sees These Enemies: How to Discern and Disarm Unseen Tempters.*

Their first aim was to ruin the multiplication of God's image (Genesis 3). But satan's success was limited; they had sons who both worshipped God. Cain was told about the devil's second dark strategy: satan's partner Sin (Genesis 4). Despite the two early successes of darkness, a righteous line continued among mankind (Genesis 5).

Third, in Genesis 6:1–7, darkness interbred with mortal women. The mixed race of mighty giants were killed in the Flood and their disembodied spirits became the demons. God then shortened our lifespans, preventing repeat corruption of human DNA.

Claiming nations was the fourth strategy of the devil and his principalities (Genesis 10-11). The Bible reveals many elements of the unseen nation-claiming—not only by darkness, but also by God.

CHAPTER 3

BABEL

THE BIBLE'S FIRST POST-FLOOD REVELATION OF THE unseen is the Tower of Babel, in Genesis 11. Many new questions arise when we apply the Standard of Explanatory Power to such an oft-told Bible event. Trusting that God had a purpose in every word opens us to deeper fellowship with Him, as we plumb His mind.

> Come, let us build ourselves a city, and a tower whose
> top is in the heavens; let us make a name for
> ourselves, lest we be scattered abroad over the
> face of the whole earth. (Genesis 11:4)

Seeking an explanation, we ask, *Why is that there?* This quest for explanation refuses to concede that the Tower of Babel is there for no purpose. Related: why is Babel the *only* event recorded from this seminal time of history? Genesis 11 records two hundred twenty-two years between the Flood and Abram's birth. Surely other important things occurred.

On the surface, the Tower of Babel explains why there are different languages. Many are content with that explanation; they plumb the revelation no further. But what will we find if we investigate Babel further?

THE THREAT DARKNESS FELT

As outlined in Books Three and Four of the *Unseen* series, God created man to replace satan's dominion on Earth. The blessing on Adam and Eve, then Noah, would echo fearfully throughout the realm of the fallen Lucifer and his partners.

> Be fruitful and multiply; fill the earth and subdue it;
>   have dominion over the fish of the sea, over the
>   birds of the air, and over every living thing that
>   moves on the earth. (Genesis 1:28)

> So God blessed Noah and his sons, and said to them:
>   "Be fruitful and multiply, and fill the earth."
>   (Genesis 9:1)

The devil and the fallen angels cannot reproduce themselves. The fright for darkness is the human multiplication of God's image. Each of the first four strategies addresses this.

But satan's problem didn't go away after the Flood. Imagine the enemies' dismay at the fast-growing population of their replacements. Human unity further aggravated the threat.

By dis-unifying the humans, satan and his cohorts could counter people's dominion on Earth. After all, satan and his cohorts felt themselves its proper dominators. That's why the people saw their city and tower as self-defense. They perceived that the kingdom of darkness wanted to scatter them.

UNIFIED HUMANITY

> Now the whole earth had one language and one
> speech.... And the LORD said, "Indeed the
> people are one and they all have one language."
> (Genesis 11:1, 6)

Genesis 10 is known as the Table of Nations because it relates the
people-groups into which the lineage of Noah divided. But Genesis
11 does not fall in chronological order. Its opening statement places
its events at Babel *before* Chapter 10's Table of Nations.

The whole earth denotes all humankind. No divisions existed;
they all lived in one place, *a plain in the land of Shinar*. Imagine such
a time—no language groups, no nations, no distinct cultures, every
living person in one metropolitan area. And this is not a self-flat-
tering description by the ancient historians. God reveals His own
assessment: *the people are one.*

BRAND NEW SOIL FERTILITY

A distinct before-and-after characterized the Flood, suggested as
indirect revelation by Genesis 6:1–8.

After our first parents' disobedience, their spirits died, and God
cursed the ground (Genesis 3:17). Reduced fruit, increased thorns
and thistles, and constant work would cause food scarcity even in our
time.

Severely aggravating that scarcity was human multiplication and
extreme longevity. For the 1,556 years in Genesis 5, these three
dynamics would cause intense competitive pressure for food.

Into the mix, the kingdom of darkness injected their third strategy, interbreeding with humanity. In the economy dominated by
their warlord offspring, described as *mighty giants*, life became very
cheap as the fight for survival caused wickedness.

But after the Flood, Noah's faith-action foreshadowed new soil fertility. Worshipping God before anything had grown, he sacrificed some of the newly endangered food animals. God responded with pleasure to see Noah's faith despite substantial risk. God's oath confirmed the indirectly revealed aftermath of the Flood: new fertility and new agricultural seasons.

> Then the LORD said in His heart, "I will never again
>   curse the ground for man's sake, although the
>   imagination of man's heart is evil from his youth;
>   nor will I again destroy every living thing as I
>   have done.
> "While the earth remains,
> Seedtime and harvest,
> Cold and heat,
> Winter and summer,
> And day and night
> Shall not cease." (Genesis 8:21–22)

Human life changed significantly after the Flood. Freed from curse, Earth's refreshed ground was now like a mega-fertile river delta. That's one reason God included Noah's vineyard in the record, to show the surprise potency of the replenished soil.

Post-Flood agriculture produced unexpected abundance. Competitive pressure was gone, and consumption could be leisurely. The uneaten grapes fermented. Noah was the first to become drunk, unaware of the intoxicating effect so familiar to us.

The soil yielded more food, for more people, with less effort. With less pressure to consume, new leisure arose.

BABEL AROSE FROM NEW LEISURE

Babel resulted from the newfound leisure time and its effects. Human reproduction rapidly replenished our population, beginning with Noah's three sons. With less effort to produce food from the fertile ground, the inventive qualities of God's image replaced the pre-Flood competition for scarce food.

Leisure multiplied babies who became workers, and many hands made lighter work. New technology caused more leisure which produced more from less effort.

The city of Babel, its tower, and the technology of massive construction projects resulted from these new economic dynamics. Like Him and like us, the unified humanity could imagine, engineer, and create.

NEW TECH, NEW TRUST

Then they said to one another, "Come, let us make bricks and bake them thoroughly." They had brick for stone, and they had asphalt for mortar. (Genesis 11:3)

The Tower of Babel represented a new high in social cooperation. The Bible record shows no other attempt at such a tower:

- a brand-new design,
- using brand-new technology,
- on a never-attempted scale,
- constructed by someone unknown to you,
- to reach the heavens.

A high level of mutual trust is required for the tower effort. Humanity's unity is plausibly necessary for this to occur.

But their motive raises significant questions.

BABEL AROSE FROM NEW FEAR

God had commanded Noah as He had Adam: *Be fruitful and multiply, and fill the Earth* (Genesis 1:28; 9:1). But fear arose within the growing mass of people, the same insecurity Cain had described to God. Being scattered was mortally threatening to them.

> Cain: "Surely You have driven me out this day from
> the face of the ground; I shall be hidden from
> Your face; I shall be a fugitive and a vagabond on
> the earth, and it will happen that anyone who
> finds me will kill me." (Genesis 4:14)

> People of Babel: "Come, let us build ourselves a city,
> and a tower whose top is in the heavens; let us
> make a name for ourselves, lest we be scattered
> abroad over the face of the whole earth." (Genesis
> 11:4)

Their prime motivating fear was being scattered, but by whom? The passage clearly says that this was a unified humanity, migrating to Shinar together with one speech and no people-groups.

DEMONS WERE BRAND NEW

> And they said, "Come, let us build ourselves a city,
> and a tower whose top is in the heavens; let us
> make a name for ourselves, lest we be scattered
> abroad over the face of the whole earth." (Genesis
> 11:4)

Book Four explored the Flood in great detail, concluding that today's demons are the half-breed offspring of angelic paternity and mortal maternity (Genesis 6:1-4). The outcomes recorded there show the spread of evil, the scarcity of food, and the warlord economy of survival—conditions which triggered God's plan for our lifespan reduction and the Flood.

With our paradigm of naturalistic materialism, we envision a skyscraper piercing low-hanging clouds. Such an explanation is weak; skyscrapers do not prevent scattering. The better explanation: they perceived the spirits of darkness.

After all, who was trying to scatter the unified humanity? Who had a motive to reduce and humiliate the race of men? We already know: satan. And now he had a new, huge corps of spirit-slaves he did not have before the Flood.

We know them as demons, absent in the heavenly rebellion of Revelation 12, their origin hidden right in Genesis 6:1–7.

> There were giants on the earth in those days, and also
>> afterward, when the sons of God came in to the
>> daughters of men and they bore children to
>> them. Those were the mighty men who were of
>> old, men of renown. (Genesis 6:4)

The transliterated Hebrew word *Nephilim* has prompted many theories about their identity; I believe those mighty giants became demons. The Flood physically killed their bodies. Their mortal maternity is clear, but who were their fathers, called *the sons of God?*

I believe they were the rebel angels who joined Lucifer's rebellion. With their angelic spirit-bodies, damned though they are, the ancients perceived them as semi-divine. Job's narrative of the heavenly courts distinguishes satan from these fallen angels.

> Now there was a day when the sons of God came to
>> present themselves before the LORD, and Satan
>> also came among them. (Job 1:6)

As spirit beings, these *sons of god* imparted spirits to their half-breed offspring. When they mated with human women, the children would have mortal bodies with eternal spirits. The paternity imparted spirits, and the maternity imparted bodies. These children became warlords amid food scarcity thanks to their giantism and might.

SATAN'S PRISON FOR HALF-BREEDS

These people were all killed in the Flood. Earth's warlords by their paternity, their maternity made them despised once disembodied by the Flood. They became the lowest of the low, satan's cannon fodder for individual oppression, whom we call *demons*.

The prison of satan received a visitor, Jesus, whom it could neither obstruct nor restrict. Apostle Peter describes Jesus' descent into hell and the limited time frame of people He sought.

> ...being put to death in the flesh but made alive by
> the Spirit, by whom also He went and preached
> to the spirits in prison, who formerly were
> disobedient, when once the Divine longsuffering
> waited in the days of Noah, while the ark was
> being prepared, in which a few, that is, eight
> souls, were saved through water. (1 Peter 3:18–
> 20)

Apostle Paul also reports Jesus' offer of salvation to any disembodied person who would follow Him out. After all, it was no fault of their own that their fathers were the fallen angels.

> Therefore He says:
> "When He ascended on high,
> He led captivity captive,
> And gave gifts to men."
> (Now this, "He ascended"—what does it mean but
> that He also first descended into the lower parts
> of the earth?) (Ephesians 4:8–9)

Jesus' descent into hell was clearly a rescue mission. Demons expelled by Him would plausibly meet Him again. The devil's prison was powerless against Jesus; his captives could become Jesus' captives.

Paul says some demons accepted His offer and He led them out. We know many demons refused the onetime offer. Demonic oppression continued in the Bible's report: deliverance ministry remains necessary and effective because of them.

SUDDEN HAUNTING

In our popular mind, disembodied ghosts linger in place after their violent death. If we are sensitive about haunting today, imagine the time when demons were brand new.

We know about the Flood from Genesis, which Moses wrote centuries later from God's revelation at Sinai. But at Babel's time, Noah was still living. The Flood was still news, not legend—the sole connection to all pre-Flood humanity.

The tales would echo around every cook-fire: the cursed ground and difficulty of food production, the warlord economy run by devilish half-breeds, and the competition for scarce food. For the people of Babel, the Flood would feel like our parents telling us about World War II or Desert Storm.

But what happened to all the mighty giants, eternal spirits now disembodied? Their spirits lived on, far outnumbering the newly replenished human population. The thought alone would frighten. It's plausible to think that the people of Babel had actual encounters with these new haunters.

If so, how could people resist them? After all, the condition of humanity was spiritual poverty and inadequacy, dead in spirit since Adam. Against disembodied half-breeds and fallen angels, fright would be disabling.

The scatterers were so dreaded because the unified people perceived them as human-haters in the unseen realm. As with any common enemy, people unified and erected their defenses: a city with a tower in the heavens.

It's easy to imagine the people's choice to remain willfully blind to such a catastrophic event and God's hand in it, because we do it as well today.

Babel is the only event between the Flood and Abraham; it's the Bible's window on humanity's spiritual perception. With the curtain on the unseen lifted, they protected themselves.

THE TOWER OF SELF-RELIANCE

Yet completely absent is any recognition of God's engagement on Earth, most recently to eradicate those half-breeds in the Flood.

The defensive actions considered by the unified humanity are just like the self-defense choice which satan offered to Adam and Eve (Genesis 3:5–6):

- God is not on our side.
- He cannot be counted on.
- We have to take care of ourselves.

That willful self-protection required three disdains for God. First, they did not trust God to protect them. Despite stories about the trust and faith of Noah, the people adopted the premise satan had suggested to Eve: "God takes care of Himself and you have to take care of yourself."

Second, self-reliance against well-practiced evil spirits could not succeed. It doomed the tower to fail. To think their meager tower and city could oppose satan's kingdom was another disdain for God.

Third, by remaining stationary in a concentrated population, the unified humanity disdained God's mandate to Noah: *fill the Earth*.

Their unified decision only *implies* their disdain for God. Their leadership conversation neither mentions Him nor challenges Him. Technically, their motive and their plan are godless, as if God doesn't even exist. The self-doing plans of human leadership discounted human history before the Flood.

The tower is godly in one way: *Let us.* The unified Trinity had started the six twenty-four-hour days of Genesis 1 with the same two words. Even ignoring the Lord God, Babel's people cannot help but express His image, nor can we.

The question remains, what benefit did they think a tower would provide?

SELF-DEFENSE

Self-defense against unseen spirits best explains the tower's motive and method. Perceiving the fallen rebels, people's inadequacy against them would be palpable. People planned to become a feared quantity against the panoply of spirit beings with their structure: *Let us make a name for ourselves.*

A tower in the heavens would make Babel a player of improved standing versus the perceptible spirits of darkness. It was not a defense against people, because unified humanity had no human enemies. But how would its top in the heavens would do that?

STRENGTH IN NUMBERS

The tower was not the limit of the architects' plans. It would stand in the middle of a new city, a walled community where proximity to other people brought safety against the frightening unseen.

The motivated belief in Genesis 11:4 is that unity gave them standing among the unseen spirits, and defended against their pressure to scatter. They believed themselves safer against unseen malevolence if they were together.

THE TOWER FOR PRIESTS

The point of the tower was to have standing among the unseen beings. No height nor cloud penetration offered that. For the host of heaven, it needn't be the tallest; *the heavens* they sought was not the sky.

Instead, the tower enabled them to contest in the heavens of the unseen realm. We are told nothing about the tower's design. Presumably, their structure had to support human movement from the bottom to the top.

The tower and its pinnacle would be a center of religious activity, repeatedly found in history. Religious actions planned for that tower would quell the scattering influence of demons.

Who would ascend upon its completion? It wasn't a tourist destination for its builders to visit with their family. Instead, a priesthood and their rituals would represent mankind in the array of beings, seen and unseen.

Jesus Himself was such a priest, designated to intercede in the heavens for people.

> For every high priest taken from among men is
>   appointed for men in things pertaining to God,
>   that he may offer both gifts and sacrifices for
>   sins. He can have compassion on those who are
>   ignorant and going astray, since he himself is also
>   subject to weakness. Because of this he is required
>   as for the people, so also for himself, to offer sac-
>   rifices for sins. (Hebrews 5:1–3)

The people of Babel lacked Noah's heart of obedience to the LORD. They sensed pressure to scatter originating in the unseen, and they wanted to oppose it with protective sacrifices and other activities on the tower.

ACTIVITIES ON THE TOWER

History shows the defensive rituals that priests enact for standing in the unseen. Archaeology has unearthed many pyramids used for human sacrifice. The deceptive whispers of satan's minions have always given rise to pagan blood-thirst. The 2006 movie *Apocalypto* graphically depicts human sacrifices.

Towers and temples were centers for sexual religious rites. Sooth-sayers read omens such as animal entrails and bones. Being lifted above ground-level humidity assisted with astrological readings and fortune-telling.

Humanity has always felt the need for such rituals and believed them effective in the spirit world. The historical record does not flatter our race, so poor in spirit yet unwilling to rely on God.

GOD'S ASSESSMENT

> Indeed the people are one and they all have one
> language, and this is what they begin to do; now
> nothing that they propose to do will be withheld
> from them. (Genesis 11:6)

God's outlook on humanity's unity is striking. Didn't He want them to succeed against unseen evil spirits, to have standing in the unseen? After all, He created us to replace satan and his henchmen. Was He not in favor of their oneness and their unified effort?

Yes, but not in the way of Babel.

Today, the democratization of information appears to unify us, yet those at the levers of power are more unassailable than ever. In contrast, we have a tower that Solomon described: *The name of the Lord is a strong tower; the righteous run to it and are safe* (Proverbs 18:10).

Jesus' nine sequential beatitudes describe the tower God blesses:

the poor in spirit, the mourning, the meek, the hungering and thirsting for righteousness, and their associated qualities (Matthew 5:1–12).

If the people of Babel had achieved their aim, would those qualities have resulted? Clearly not. In their place would be a self-deceived, satanic, and narcissistic human pride. A controlling priesthood would be a chokepoint of the few, enabling the competing principalities to rule the many.

Dictating the sacrifices necessary to justify their control, the priests of the tower would be the *haves*. Everyone else would be the *have-nots*—a social stratification with no escape.

LANGUAGE = GROUP

New languages required new vocal muscles and vocabularies instantly. Also sudden: an understanding of a few other people, and inability to learn the other languages.

God's solution was to *dis-unify* people. That's why He divided them into language-groups, the first in human history. Ethnicity has been with us ever since.

> "Come, let Us go down and there confuse their
> language, that they may not understand one
> another's speech." So the LORD scattered them
> abroad from there over the face of all the earth,
> and they ceased building the city. Therefore its
> name is called Babel, because there the LORD
> confused the language of all the earth; and from
> there the LORD scattered them abroad over the
> face of all the earth. (Genesis 11:7-9).

Never had there been ethnic groups or distinct cultures—but they have been with us ever since. Today, race and ethnicity are perpetually hot topics. Injustice often lies along the fault lines between people-groups. Different language groups have produced unique cultures and morphed into politically bounded nations.

The result of God's action was exactly what the once-unified humans dreaded: scattering. *From there the LORD scattered them abroad over the face of all the earth* (Genesis 11:9).

Elsewhere in the *Unseen* Series

Book Four, *Nobody Sees These Enemies: How to Discern and Disarm Unseen Tempters,* thoroughly considered God's language action described in Genesis 11. The brief passage makes direct statements, and also implies what enables those statements.

GOD SCATTERED

We acutely feel our need for security against the unholy unseen, because we are indeed poor in spirit. But it has never come by human unity, because God irresistibly divided and scattered humanity.

Their godlessness left God out of the equation, as modern society does. When He re-inserted Himself, no tower could prevent it. They were right to fear scattering by spirits. It was an unseen spirit that did it: God.

UNIFIED IN THE LAST DAYS

The Bible tells us that the human unity of Genesis 11 will return. Matthew 24 is Jesus' prophecy about the end times.

> Then they will deliver you up to tribulation and kill
>   you, and you will be hated by all nations for My
>   name's sake. And then many will be offended, will

betray one another, and will hate one another.
Then many false prophets will rise up and deceive
many. And because lawlessness will abound, the
love of many will grow cold. (Matthew 24:9–12)

Humanity will unify, Jesus said: against us who love Him.
Mourning His appearance will also unify them when He comes on
the clouds in power and great glory (Matthew 24:30–31).

In the book of Revelation, multiple events depict a humanity
unified against the kingdom of God and His people. Apostle John
witnesses the end of the world in three cycles of revelation. Each cycle
includes a unified humanity: mourning for their helplessness against
God, refusing to repent, and raging against His kingdom.

And the kings of the earth, the great men, the rich
men, the commanders, the mighty men, every
slave and every free man, hid themselves in the
caves and in the rocks of the mountains, and said
to the mountains and rocks, "Fall on us and hide
us from the face of Him who sits on the throne
and from the wrath of the Lamb! For the great
day of His wrath has come, and who is able to
stand?" (Revelation 6:15–17)

But the rest of mankind, who were not killed by these
plagues, did not repent of the works of their
hands, that they should not worship demons,
and idols of gold, silver, brass, stone, and wood,
which can neither see nor hear nor walk. And
they did not repent of their murders or their
sorceries or their sexual immorality or their
thefts. (Revelation 9:20–21)

Those who dwell on the earth will rejoice over them

[the two witnesses], make merry, and send gifts
to one another, because these two prophets
tormented those who dwell on the earth. (Revelation 11:10)

THE REASON FOR ISRAEL

Babel is far more than a random, interesting story. The new, distinct
groups are the foundation for God's call to Abraham and later choice
of Israel as His peculiar people.

The rapid rise of *ethnos* people-groups also gave the kingdom of
darkness an opportunity. The devil could now economize his
control, as we will see in Section 2, *Nation-Claiming*.

A principality of darkness claimed each language group, one
fallen angel the unseen king over each group. Darkness could rule the
many through the few.

If God did nothing else, that single statement would describe all
human history forever. But He entered the free-for-all and claimed
one for Himself. It's as if God said, "Claiming nations, are you? Well,
I'll claim one too."

The entire Old Testament is based on this. The explanatory
power is profound for your walk with God and life on Earth. His call
began with Abraham.

CHAPTER 4

ABRAHAM

IN SETH'S LINE, ENOCH THEN NOAH INTERACTED WITH the spirit realm, namely with God Himself. Noah was the first man Scripture describes as righteous.

Not until Abram does righteousness return to the forefront. He is also the next one named with exposure to the unseen. The primary spirit whom Abram encountered was God Himself. The first legacy deposit into a family line, by the unseen God, was righteousness.

HE HEARD GOD

God's unique dealings with Abram begin with one potent statement: *Now the LORD had said to Abram* (Genesis 12:1). This became habitual, a repeated conversational intimacy.

> The LORD appeared to Abram... And the LORD
> said to Abram, after Lot had separated from
> him... The word of the LORD came to Abram in
> a vision... the word of the LORD came to him...
> The LORD made a covenant with Abram,

saying... the LORD appeared to Abram and said
to him... Then the LORD appeared to him...
(Genesis 12:7, 13:14, 15:1,4,18, 17:1, 18:1)

That is only a sampling. In a soliloquy, revealed and recorded for
our hearing, YHWH describes His attitude to the man He renamed
Abraham

And the LORD said, "Shall I hide from Abraham
what I am doing, since Abraham shall surely
become a great and mighty nation, and all the
nations of the earth shall be blessed in him? For I
have known him..." (Genesis 18:17–19)

HE BELIEVED GOD

God did not relate to Abraham based on obedience to the Law,
which came many centuries later. Righteousness is unearned, a spiritual reward for believing God. Faith rather than works is the basis—
just as it is for us who follow Jesus Christ in faith.

And he believed in the LORD, and He accounted it
to him for righteousness. (Genesis 15:6, cf.
Romans 4:13)

But now the righteousness of God apart from the law
is revealed..., through faith in Jesus Christ, to
all and on all who believe. (Romans 3:21–22)

Abraham's life defines the righteousness God imparted to him
and the nation he produced. It was a legacy deposit, uniquely available to his descendants. Through Isaac and Jacob, then David and his
line, Jesus ultimately inherited the righteousness.

> When He suffered, He did not threaten, but commit-
> ted Himself to Him who judges righteously; who
> Himself bore our sins in His own body on the
> tree, that we, having died to sins, might live for
> righteousness—by whose stripes you were healed.
> (1 Peter 2:23–24)

WHAT IS RIGHTEOUSNESS?

In the Bible languages, the word for *righteousness* has a comprehen-
sive *con*notation, rather than a limited technical *de*notation.

Behaviors evidence righteousness, but are not the main signal.
People can *behave* righteously. We can be loving and good. Useful
personal traits—intelligence, character, talents—benefit many others.

But righteousness is a spiritual impartation. Only God can give it,
and He alone is its measure. Righteousness with people and things is
an overflow of God's righteousness. Its source in an unseen Spirit
makes it an unseen quality.

Only humans can manifest righteousness, which requires a free
will. Relationships with persons are the arena, without excluding
animals and Earth.

Like it or not, God Almighty is the primary Person in all our
lives. The foundation of righteousness is your elective relationship
with Him. He alone is the reference point of righteousness.

That's how Apostle Paul can distinguish goodness and righteousness in Romans 5:7.

> For scarcely for a righteous man will one die; yet
> perhaps for a good man someone would even
> dare to die.

RIGHTEOUSNESS RE-INTRODUCED

The Bible record before the Flood identifies only three men as righteous: Abel, Enoch and Noah. It didn't matter to humanity at Babel, godless in their thinking and plans.

But two hundred years after the Flood, the LORD re-introduced the unseen qualities of righteousness on Earth through Abraham.

> For I have known him, in order that he may
>   command his children and his household after
>   him, that they keep the way of the LORD, to do
>   righteousness and justice, that the LORD may
>   bring to Abraham what He has spoken to him.
>   (Genesis 18:19)

RIGHTEOUSNESS TO SEE UNSEEN

Through Abraham, God introduced a line of authority on Earth, enabling us to perceive the unseen realm reliably and truthfully. The Old Testament proceeded from that legacy authority. That's why it repeatedly lifts the curtain on the unseen, for both Israelites and Gentiles.

After Jesus performed His reconciling work, we could all be righteous with God, not only a few. So He released *far more* unveiling by pouring out the holiest Spirit of them all. That's who now lives within you and each born-again Christian. When you read Scripture, every deposit YHWH placed there is being read by His Spirit within you.

Yet even we can choose willful blindness to the unseen. How can we overcome that wicked habit of limiting what we see? Scripture repeatedly tells us: meekness.

> For thus says the High and Lofty One
> Who inhabits eternity, whose name *is* Holy:

"I dwell in the high and holy *place*,
With him *who* has a contrite and humble spirit,
To revive the spirit of the humble,
And to revive the heart of the contrite ones." (Isaiah
57:15)

TRAINING IN RIGHTEOUSNESS

Because righteousness is an impartation from the unseen, God has to tutor us. His first tutoring in the Bible was in Eden; Adam's animal-naming was training to love Eve.

The destruction of Sodom was God's judgment on sin, but we wrongly limit the event to that alone. Through it, He also tutors Abraham about His righteousness.

Read below what God said to Abraham; He did not say what would happen to the evil cities. But Abraham perceived the innuendo that destruction was pending for the cities where his nephew Lot lived.

> And the LORD said, "Because the outcry against
> Sodom and Gomorrah is great, and because
> their sin is very grave, I will go down now and
> see whether they have done altogether
> according to the outcry against it that has come
> to Me; and if not, I will know." (Genesis
> 18:20–21)

In a purposeful conversation, God trains Abraham to see reality through the grid of righteousness.

> And Abraham came near and said, "Would You also
> destroy the righteous with the wicked? Suppose
> there were fifty righteous within the city; would
> You also destroy the place and not spare *it* for the

fifty righteous that were in it? (Genesis 18:23–24)

God's apparent negotiation with Abraham resembles Jesus' apparent negotiation with the Syro-Phoenician woman in Mark 7:24–30. The words of the Lord mask an opposite intent, and the negotiating person had to perceive more than the words. In the sick daughter's case, Jesus's harsh-sounding speech tutored the mother in faith because He wanted to heal the daughter.

Likewise, the LORD knew the condition of Sodom would cause its destruction; He did not need Abraham's endorsement. Each request Abraham made lowered the numerical threshold for sparing the city, and God honored each one. He was tutoring the father of many nations about a fundamental quality of the unseen: righteousness.

> Far be it from You to do such a thing as this, to slay
> the righteous with the wicked, so that the right-
> eous should be as the wicked; far be it from You!
> Shall not the Judge of all the earth do right?
> (Genesis 18:25)

INHERITABLE RIGHTEOUSNESS

The call of Abraham differed from all of God's previous interaction with people. Never since He punished Adam and Eve had His action affected an entire lineage, not even Seth's line. When Yahweh singled out Abram in the city of Ur, it was completely new in His dealing with mankind.

He was calling one family lineage to be His people. God claimed an *ethnos* nation.

CHAPTER 5

THE NAME OF GOD

MOSES RECEIVED GOD'S REVELATION OF HIS OFFICIAL name in the first encounter at the burning bush. The curtain lifted, Moses would also see God walk past and hear God declare His qualities. God's Bible name helps you understand the Old Testament and its revelation of the unseen realm.

> And God said to Moses, "I AM WHO I AM." And
> He said, "Thus you shall say to the children of
> Israel, 'I AM has sent me to you.'" ... This is My
> name forever, and this is My memorial to all
> generations." (Exodus 3:14–15)

In English, God's name is actually an entire phrase: *I am who I am*. Why is it capitalized? Why doesn't it appear throughout the English-language Old Testament—especially if it is His name forever? And why don't we see it in the New Testament?

USING GOD'S NAME

Vowels were not used in Hebrew writing. The English phrase *I am who I am* translates only four Hebrew consonants, YHWH (in our alphabet). The four letters are called the tetragrammaton, from the Greek word meaning "four letters."

Moses wrote the Law in proto-Hebrew. See my wife Diane's book, *Is the Bible Even Real? Who Knew?* In every-day language (without footnotes) she tells how the Bible's history affirms its trustworthiness.

To avoid violating the third commandment not to take God's name in vain, Jewish religious regulators would not use it at all. Such misplaced reverence explains their response to Jesus, who not only spoke it, but identified Himself by it. Note the capitalization.

Jesus said to them, "Most assuredly, I say to you,
    before Abraham was, I AM." Then they took up
    stones to throw at Him... (John 8:57–58)

However, God's name was throughout the scriptures they copied and debated. So when they had to refer to it, the Jewish scribes substituted another Hebrew word: *Adonai*, meaning Lord in the same way we address people in English as Sir, Master, or Boss.

TRANSLATING GOD'S NAME

The tradition of avoiding God's revealed name persists in Hebrew translation. In English translators still substitute *the LORD* when YHWH appears in the Old Testament. Wherever you see *The LORD* in the Old Testament, you can read the actual Hebrew name, *Yahweh*, which in English means *I AM THAT I AM*.

That tradition of substitution is waning. Increasingly, Christians welcome the Old Testament name *Yahweh*, the traditional vocalized sound of the four consonants.

A variation arose after the German reformer Martin Luther, *Jehovah,* with a first letter pronunciation like our word *joy*. Their letter J sounds like the English language Y. German scholars also added the vowels differently.

The accepted practice now is to pronounce the four Hebrew consonants YHWH with a breathy sound over a fricative H, not the fricative J and V sound as our alphabet requires. We pronounce the tetragrammaton with a soft exhale: *Yah-weh*.

YHWH is Jehovah is I AM WHO I AM is the LORD *is the Triune God.* These pages often follow the tradition by writing *the* LORD. It's also spelled out, Yahweh. You'll also see *I AM WHO I AM,* as well as the abbreviated *I AM*.

GOD'S NAME AMONG NATIONS

Cross-*ethnos* interactions were people's competitive arena for the most powerful god, not unlike our fandom for sports teams. Nations construed their military success as a validation for the supremacy of their divinity.

But the name YHWH is only the wind of an exhale. That's a reason that wind and spirit are the same word in both the Old and New Testaments. Wind is anything but militaristic.

Yahweh's chosen name distinguished Him from the gods of other nations: Milcom, Chemosh, Baal, Ashtoreth, Jupiter, and Juno (to name only a few). Pagan gods had specific assignments and duties. Baal was the god of agricultural fertility; Mars was the god of Roman military might. But I AM THAT I AM expresses no assignment.

History and Scripture have shown the pagan gods were the tran-

THE NAME OF GOD

sient public face of the unseen principalities. One god is permanent, one only: I AM.

FREEDOM IN THE I AM

Why would God choose such a name as *I AM THAT I AM?* One reason: He relates to reality on a NOW basis. God is not subject to time; the spirit world is an eternal NOW for His kingdom. We can only interact with Him in His NOW, whatever our time may be.

In contrast, we easily let the past linger. Its tendrils aggressively attach to our present life, and spoil our future. Guilt is an example; its origin is always in the past. Likewise, the past accusations of others can cling to your self-image, whether true or false. And our enemies continually use God's holiness to curse your future.

> ...the accuser of our brethren, who accused them
> before our God day and night. (Revelation
> 12:10)

I AM names His freedom from past and future. YHWH means He relates to us in the present, not limited by our past or future. God's name assures His followers that the present moment is a safe place. Only you can import the foreign elements of past and present.

CONFESSION IN THE I AM

In fact, we do import them into God's safe NOW. The accusations are worse even than we know.

But repentance severs the lingering grip of the past and the stormy haunt of the future. Until our death, we can confess and repent, unlike the fallen angels. Both our Latin-derived *confess* and the Bible's Greek word *homologeo* mean to *say the same,* whether about action, thought, speech, or desire.

God, I say the same that You do about my past offense. I also agree that Jesus died in my place for that sin. Therefore, I announce for all the heavens to hear, Your justice to Jesus accepts His substitution for me and imparts His righteousness. I break and forsake any agreement(s) with enemies using that sin against You and me.

We can also repent of worry and pride, which bring the future into the present. Jesus specifically targeted that.

> Therefore do not worry about tomorrow, for tomorrow will worry about its own things. Sufficient for the day is its own trouble. (Matthew 6:34)

Lord God, I agree with You, and accept that I am safe right now with You. I entrust my future to Your management and will obey what You assign to my care in the NOW.

Coming pages show that a fallen angel promotes common sins throughout your *ethnos*. God knows it and will judge them for it. Confession and repentance are your responsibility, and free you from the ethnic grip.

When we *say the same* with the I AM WHO I AM, He liberates us for the NOW, out of our people-group's past and future.

JACOB AND THE NAME

Jacob was Abraham's grandson; his name meant supplanter. You could not have a more vivid spiritual encounter than he did.

It happened in his most delicate survival situation. Reunion with his alienated brother, Esau, threatened a total loss of life and wealth. Jacob's supplanter character hoped his family and possessions would exhaust Esau's hatred. Sending them ahead in stages, Jacob left himself last in the procession and alone.

But the unexpected happened. The Incarnate Jesus, the NOW of God, appeared on Jacob's night alone and physically wrestled him.

> Then Jacob was left alone; and a Man wrestled with
> him until the breaking of day. Now when He saw
> that He did not prevail against him, He touched
> the socket of his hip; and the socket of Jacob's
> hip was out of joint as He wrestled with him.
> (Genesis 32:24–25)

Picturing the dramatic match, we might focus on the pending survival threat from Esau. Encountering God today, people would think of questions to pursue, favors to ask, or enemies to curse. Jacob's focus is much different: the Man's name.

> Then Jacob asked, saying, "Tell me Your name, I
> pray."
> And He said, "Why is it that you ask about My
> name?" And He blessed him there.
> So Jacob called the name of the place Peniel: "For I
> have seen God face to face, and my life is
> preserved." (Genesis 32:29-30)

Only later to Moses would God reveal His name, not to Jacob. Instead, Jacob had to yield his name to the Man, who renamed him with this diagnostic prophecy.

> Your name shall no longer be called Jacob, but Israel;

for you have struggled with God and with men,
and have prevailed. (Genesis 32:28)

The family of twelve sons would become the nation we know today, named by God for their wrestling with God and man.

PART TWO

NATION-CLAIMING

In addition to the Bible paradigm of spirits, a paradigm of people-groups is also required. The spirits of the unseen realm deal with the nations, languages, and cultures of people.

Apostle Paul didn't write, *I wrestle not against flesh and blood*. You are part of Paul's God-inspired sentence: *We wrestle*. We can perceive and wrestle in the spirit world we now inhabit.

Like Paul, we must recognize the principalities, rulers, and spiritual forces of wickedness in the heavenly realms. Apostle John said *test the spirits*, because we live among them.

We read the Bible with our American individualism. But to understand God's choice of Israel and His salvation of mankind, we must learn the Bible paradigm of *ethnos* nations. In the coming pages, you'll learn satan's ethnic system: corrupting many through few.

The Bible's *ethnos* will impart to you a vital understanding of our true enemies.

CHAPTER 6

HOW NATION-CLAIMING WORKS

THE DEVIL WANTS GOD TO REJECT THE RACE OF MEN, HIS own image-creatures. But our fruitful reproduction outstrips their created capacity.

For maximum output and ruthless efficiency, the subordinates of darkness deal with groups of people. This reduces the number satan requires, from billions to hundreds. The devil's prison of Isaiah 14:17 has to parole fewer partners.

God is also a spirit, and He works with groups of people as well. Scripture names many as well as Israel. He scatters people at Babel, destroys Sodom, and repeatedly punishes the peoples of the Levant. In these Bible actions, Yahweh is dealing not with individuals but with *ethnos*.

DANIEL SAW IT

King Nebuchadnezzar elevated Daniel and three other Jewish exiles to a court vantage point. They witnessed the unseen competition of divinities—including the LORD—throughout the known world, which even pagan kings acknowledged. Daniel's book is like Yahweh's sports-victory highlight reel (emphasis mine).

> Therefore I make a decree that **any people, nation, or language** which speaks anything amiss against the God of Shadrach, Meshach, and Abed-Nego shall be cut in pieces, and their houses shall be made an ash heap; because there is no other God who can deliver like this. (Nebuchadnezzar in Daniel 3:29)

> Nebuchadnezzar the king, **to all peoples, nations, and languages** that dwell in all the earth: Peace be multiplied to you. I thought it good to declare the signs and wonders that the Most High God has worked for me. (Nebuchadnezzar in Daniel 4:1)

> O king, the Most High God gave Nebuchadnezzar your father a kingdom and majesty, glory and honor. And because of the majesty that He gave him, **all peoples, nations, and languages** trembled and feared before him. (Daniel to Belshazzar in Daniel 5:18–19)

> King Darius wrote: **To all peoples, nations, and languages** that dwell in all the earth: Peace be multiplied to you. I make a decree that in every dominion of my kingdom men must tremble and fear before the God of Daniel. (Darius in Daniel 6:25–26)

> Behold, One like the Son of Man, coming with the clouds of heaven! He came to the Ancient of

Days, and they brought Him near before Him.
Then to Him was given dominion and glory and
a kingdom, **that all peoples, nations, and
languages should serve Him**. (Daniel's vision
in 7:13–14)

The competing spirits became clear to Daniel. Bible revelation becomes far clearer to us as well, by accepting that both Yahweh and the partners of satan interact with us in our *ethnos* groups. Everything in the Old Testament becomes far more clear if the spirits of the unseen interact with people's groupings.

The claiming of the nations provided the perfect strategy for darkness. The Old Testament is the record of God's responses to them. But how did principalities make their claims on people-groups? By answering that, we can discern the unseen rulers today and release their captives more effectively.

The answer is in the Bible's implications. Let's reverse engineer from God's direct revelation.

DARKNESS OWNS THE KINGDOMS

In Luke 4:5-7, we read satan's effort to induce Jesus to sin.

The devil led him up to a high place and showed him
in an instant all the kingdoms of the world. And
he said to him, "I will give you all their authority
and splendor; it has been given to me, and I can
give it to anyone I want to. If you worship me, it
will all be yours."

Jesus did not dispute satan's claim. His response accepts what satan said: the nations and kingdoms of the world really are satan's to give. But how were the kingdoms given to satan, and by whom? Many have debated this with different responses.

Jesus wasn't seeing their geographical territories, an impossibility. I believe the kingdoms were not citizens nor territories, but their unseen rulers. To infiltrate and ensnare humanity, the devil gives his fellow rebels authority over the *ethnos*. They congregated at their master's summons, in debt to satan for all their authority.

That's why Jesus could see all the kingdoms from one high place. He was seeing the principalities whom satan had summoned.

How did these unseen kings dominate the world's *ethnos*? By the process of nation-claiming or *ethnos*-claiming.

SATAN'S HENCHMEN

Exiled from heaven together with the fallen Lucifer, a third of heaven's angels swore fealty to him, like feudal lords. He became satan but retained his sway over them. As the source of all their power and authority, he can replace, demote, and promote them as he wishes.

As Seen Yesterday & Today

Feudalism in Western civilization & warlords in developing countries today mimic the hierarchical IOU system in the kingdom of darkness. From English heritage, it is well-demonstrated in the history of the monarchy and its land grants.

This feudal IOU system was portrayed in the movie *Braveheart*; the Scotch lords betrayed William Wallace because King Edward gave them lands.

In Isaiah 14:9-10, God reveals the relationship between satan and his nation-ruling subordinates.

The realm of the dead below is all astir
to meet you at your coming;
it rouses the spirits of the departed to greet you—

all those who were leaders in the world;
it makes them rise from their thrones—
all those who were kings over the nations.
They will all respond,
they will say to you,
"You also have become weak, as we are;
you have become like us."

COMMON SIN THROUGH THE FEW

By influencing the leaders of an *ethnos*, the assigned principality could induce the entire people-group to sin in common ways. Consider the faults of nations and ethnic groups today; common sins run in them clearly.

Each group inherits a legacy of unique sin; stereotypes represent its reputation impact. We don't lump everyone into a stereotype, but our antennae go up. Common reputation may signify common patterns of excused sin.

I have heard the following stereotypes over fifty years of ministry and business. Do they signal a sin regarded as acceptable by most of that group? If so, their unseen ruler was the instigator. (Full disclosure: I am a white American Southerner of Scotch origin.)

- Italians: hotheaded and reactionary
- Germans: analytical and methodical
- Irish: drunks and witches
- Scotch: stubborn and warlike
- English: domineering and self-superior
- French: lovers
- Jews: cheaters
- Nigerians: swindlers
- South Africans: racists
- Latinos: excitable and irrational
- Indians: liars

- Japanese: duplicitous backstabbers
- Russians: alcoholics
- Chinese: devious supplanters
- Americans: self-centered and arrogant.
- Whites: unjust and oppressive
- Blacks: lazy and uneducated
- American Indians: impetuous drunkards
- Californians: self-indulgent
- New Yorkers: rude
- Southerners: stupid
- Wall Street: rapacious and greedy
- Politicians and attorneys: lying hypocrites
- Evangelists: adulterous fame-seeking hucksters

That's only a few people-groups. Every *ethnos* earns its own stereotype fair and square; they are not without a basis in reality. God warned in Exodus 20:5 that the sins of the fathers are visited on the children.

The dread of darkness was the multiplication of God's reproducing image on Earth. But they learned how to reproduce a common sin pattern and thus separate an entire *ethnos* from God. The kingdom of darkness still cements common iniquitous patterns in family lines. Sin, rather than righteousness, becomes the legacy deposit. The resulting sin pattern magnetizes the heredity of the *ethnos* and gives rise to stereotypes.

MASTERS OF PUPPET KINGS

The principality controls the people-group through its leaders. Bribes of wealth, pleasure, fame, or power hook the leader. Once under the grip of darkness, God's light becomes fearsome to these influencers. The evil ruler can then threaten the leader with that light: exposure, shame, and loss of position.

The devil, the unseen puppet master, and the human leader form a hierarchy that imposes a group's sin into each of its children.

On his missionary journeys, Apostle Paul penetrated one *ethnos* after another. He encountered this ethnic reality repeatedly and identified who we wrestle with. He only mentions the devil for his strategic schemes. Only three people in the Bible had direct dealings with the devil; it's the henchmen we wrestle.

> We do not wrestle against flesh and blood, but
> against principalities, against powers, against the
> rulers of the darkness of this age, against spiritu-
> al hosts of wickedness in the heavenly places.
> (Ephesians 6:12)

ONLY ONE INIQUITY NEEDED

The group's people still have the qualities of God's image-creatures. A spiritual force of wickedness doesn't have to introduce every sin into its *ethnos*, nor prohibit good deeds.

The unseen ruler would benefit from meritorious human developments. When its *ethnos* becomes prominent among nations, the principality would gain prestige within the kingdom of darkness. In addition, the sin-pattern indulged by its pet people becomes influential on other people-groups.

The unseen ruler only needs one familial sin, one common offense against the Creator. Following their leaders, the people of the *ethnos* adopt the sin and excuse it.

Voilé, the entire nation allies with darkness. With this claim system, the limited number of fallen angels is not at the mercy of human reproduction. By ruining each language-family that God created at Babel, they could make all humanity odious to God. His own image-creature would be in alliance with darkness, even unwittingly.

INHERITABLE INIQUITY

Once an *ethnos* is a slave to its unseen king, latent agreements with darkness await all its babies. Baked into the culture is inheritable iniquity, and its children are born in thrall to twisted dark rulers. An Abel, an Enoch, a Noah could arise within the group, but only by the action and preservation of God.

The prophet Balaam illustrates this in Numbers 22. God interacted with him, and he was an accurate prophet; all that Balaam foretold has occurred. Yet Balaam couldn't escape the kingdom of darkness; his love of profit over obedience condemned him. He stands as a pattern of all such people.

> They have forsaken the right way and gone astray,
>> following the way of Balaam the son of Beor,
>> who loved the wages of unrighteousness. (2 Peter 2:15)

MANIPULATED JUDGMENT

All the heavenly host knows God must judge righteously. Abraham knew it as well from his conversation about Sodom (Genesis 18). The kingdom of darkness uses God's holiness against people.

That's why principalities weave a sin-pattern into their *ethnos* people-group. It forces God's hand of holy judgment against the very creature made in His image.

CHAPTER 7

THE OLD TESTAMENT PEOPLES

THE WISDOM IN APOSTLE PAUL'S EPISTLES WAS HARD-
earned from the nation-claimers' push-back. Almost none of the
following are recorded in the book of Acts.

> From the Jews five times I received forty stripes
>   minus one. Three times I was beaten with rods;
>   once I was stoned; three times I was shipwrecked;
>   a night and a day I have been in the deep; in jour-
>   neys often, in perils of waters, in perils of
>   robbers, in perils of my own countrymen, in
>   perils of the Gentiles, in perils in the city, in perils
>   in the wilderness, in perils in the sea, in perils
>   among false brethren; in weariness and toil, in
>   sleeplessness often, in hunger and thirst, in fast-
>   ings often, in cold and nakedness... (2
>   Corinthians 11:22–27)

But the gospel's spread in Acts clearly concurs with Paul's
description of unseen rulers. The gospel's obstacles in each territory

evidenced that unique spiritual kings ruled them. That's who we wrestle against.

Once Apostle Paul learned about the control of principalities, he found it in his Scripture, our Old Testament.

THE OLD TESTAMENT THEIR BIBLE

Jesus and the apostles did not have the New Testament. The only Bible in which Jesus could see Himself was our Old Testament. Despite modern disdain, it is not outdated; it contains the gospel that gave birth to the New Testament.

Four apostles (Paul, Peter, Matthew, and John) and several others wrote our New Testament. All cite the older scriptures extensively. Their thinking was thoroughly Old Testament. Jesus explained His ministry using it.

Yes, they had to grapple with the purpose of the Law, but far from discarding it, they dove into it. Guess who they found there? Jesus.

> Did not our heart burn within us while He talked
> with us on the road, and while He opened the
> Scriptures to us?... Then He said to them, "These
> are the words which I spoke to you while I was
> still with you, that all things must be fulfilled
> which were written in the Law of Moses and the
> Prophets and the Psalms concerning Me." And
> He opened their understanding, that they might
> comprehend the Scriptures. (Luke 24: 32, 44–
> 45)

THE PEOPLE-GROUPS

After God's division of humanity at Babel, our multiplication caused new people-groups. Genesis 10 is called *The Table of Nations,* because it lists seventy separate nations descended from Noah's three sons, Shem, Ham, and Japheth.

The ancestor's name often became the name of the land. Before *Egypt* was its most well-known name, the land of the Nile was called *Cush* after the son of Ham (10:6). That's what it was called in the description of Eden's rivers (2:13). A son of Cush, Nimrod, returned to the land of Shinar and its incomplete tower to found the Assyrian capital city, Nineveh (10:11).

Ham had another son named Canaan whose land received his name (Genesis 10:16–18). But the LORD overrides that with His promise to Abram, naming several of those people groups.

> On the same day the LORD made a covenant with
>   Abram, saying:
> "To your descendants I have given this land, from the
>   river of Egypt to the great river, the River
>   Euphrates—the Kenites, the Kenezzites, the
>   Kadmonites, the Hittites, the Perizzites, the
>   Rephaim, the Amorites, the Canaanites, the
>   Girgashites, and the Jebusites." (Genesis 15:18-
>   21)

THE ANCIENT IDOLS WERE SPIRITS

After God's language separation at Babel, spirits were still perceptible. The self-defense motive still existed. People had to mollify the unseen rulers who laid claim to them.

Many ancient temples still exist. Impressive and enduring, they show the grandeur devoted to the *gods*. Hundreds of pocket-sized idols, which people carried like a rabbit's foot today, are in history museums. Sometimes ancestor worship identified the spirits as deceased people. Each group developed a unique means to honor their so-called divinity. Their religion codified the practices; thus was idolatry born.

But idolatry is not merely a sin, nor is it limited to temples and figurines. It shows that intimidating spirits are perceptible. The people-groups of immature humanity saw their welfare in pleasing them.

Five centuries after Abraham's life, Israel's general Joshua laid out a choice that all people must make. You may not realize that a principality contests God for the rulership of your *ethnos*, but that does not diminish the fact. Admonishing all Israel, Joshua described the idol worship in the land of Abraham's origin, Ur.

> Now therefore, fear the LORD, serve Him in
> sincerity and in truth, and put away the gods
> which your fathers served on the other side of the
> River and in Egypt. Serve the LORD! And if it
> seems evil to you to serve the LORD, choose for
> yourselves this day whom you will serve, whether
> the gods which your fathers served that were on
> the other side of the River, or the gods of the
> Amorites, in whose land you dwell. But as for me
> and my house, we will serve the LORD. (Joshua
> 24:14–15)

BUT IT'S OUR IDOL-SPIRIT

The assigned principality would promote an unholiness to prompt God's judgment. The group developed their culture to excuse the sin and pass it down to children. They codified the religious practices to placate the spirit-ruler. These set the ethnic identity for all other nations to see.

Loyalty to family meant loyalty to their idols. Laban shows the power of such loyalty to obscure the true God, in Genesis 31:30–35. He was the father of Jacob's wives Leah and Rachel. But he cheated Jacob, and the family fled.

The two sisters felt betrayed, and maybe entitled to some recovery. Laban had household idols, and Rachel took them from his home (31:15). Laban chased the escapees with ill intent.

But on the last night of his seven-day pursuit, God appeared and told Laban to treat Jacob with fear and respect. Yet so strong is the loyalty to the idols of our *ethnos,* even after such an encounter, the theft of his household gods is Laban's uppermost complaint.

> It is in my power to do you harm, but the God of
> your father spoke to me last night, saying, 'Be
> careful that you speak to Jacob neither good nor
> bad.' And now you have surely gone because you
> greatly long for your father's house, *but* why did
> you steal my gods? (Genesis 31:29–30)

Why would Laban prefer his idols to the LORD God Almighty, who appeared to him? Their spiritual influence was a real thing, not mere clay figurines. In coming chapters, we will review the reality of sorcery, closely related. Spirits of darkness command respect and obedience from their claimed nations.

THE NAMED DIVINITIES

The Word of God names at least fifty-four divinities, searchable at *ChristianAnswers.net.* In the ancient mindset, different gods had unique roles and requirements. For instance, Syria's attacks on Israel repeatedly failed because a prophet discerned their movements and told Israel's king. But the Syrians excused their failures by saying that Israel's god was a god of the hills (1 Kings 20:23).

Several ancient Canaanite gods maintained their influence even after Israel's conquest of Canaan. The principality Baal is a frequent Bible competitor for God's claimed *ethnos.* His feminine consort was Ashtoreth, whom other peoples called Astarte.

King Solomon passively deferred to his wives' idols. Thus, the wisest man ever to live manifested the greatest foolishness. Thanks to him, unseen forces of wickedness increased their dominion among God's people, and made Israel odious to their own God.

Why would the Israelites forsake the exclusive loyalty that Yahweh required? Why risk His ire? They believed the fertility of their land depended on placating Baal.

The worship practices centered on Baal and Ashtoreth presumed their influence on agricultural seasons, fertility, and harvests. Fertility rituals of sexual intercourse with temple prostitutes aroused the gods' sexual intercourse and ensured the coming season's harvest—or so they believed.

The disloyal Israelites worshipped the gods of several nations. Molech ruled the people of Ammon, Lot's descendants through his daughter. Child sacrifice was necessary to placate that god and secure his favor for the Ammonites.

Another *ethnos* bore the name of Lot's child by his other daughter, Moab. They worshipped Chemosh.

A Moabite king hired the false prophet Balaam to curse the migrating Israelites in Numbers 22. The king's prophetic strategy sorely backfired, but since immorality was permissible with Chemosh, Balaam advised the Moabites to seduce the Israelites sexually, and disarm the threat of conquest by Israel.

STEAL, KILL, DESTROY

The theme is clear. Every worship required by these divinities were contrary to God's loving plan for people. The fiction novelist James Michener, known for his historical research, used a people-group named Makor and their god Melak to illustrate the destruction of idolatry.

But when the god Melak was imported from the
coastal cities of the north, a new problem arose.
The citizens of Makor were eager to adopt him,

partly because his demands upon them were severe, as this proved his power, and partly because they had grown somewhat contemptuous of their local gods precisely because they had not been demanding. [Melak] had not been forced upon the town; the town had sought him our as the fulfillment of a felt need, and the more demanding he became, the more they respected him... Equally acceptable was the progression whereby Melak's appetite had expanded from the blood of a pigeon to the burning of a dead sheep to the immolation of living children, for with each extension of his appetite he became more powerful and therefore more pleasing to the people he tyrannized. (James Michener, *The Source*, pp. 133-134; New York: Dial Press/Random House, 1965)

In stark contrast stood the demands of the true God and His judgment upon the worship practices of Israel's idols. The prophet Jeremiah suffered greatly for reminding the people, right from the Temple steps.

For I did not speak to your fathers, or command them in the day that I brought them out of the land of Egypt, concerning burnt offerings or sacrifices. But this is what I commanded them, saying, 'Obey My voice, and I will be your God, and you shall be My people. And walk in all the ways that I have commanded you, that it may be well with you.' [But instead] they have built the high places of Tophet, which is in the Valley of the Son of Hinnom, to burn their sons and their daughters in the fire, which I did not command, nor did it come into My heart. (Jeremiah 7:22–23, 31)

THE IDOL-GODS WERE SPIRITS

Through the prophets of the Old Testament, God frequently revealed the masquerading "gods." Beginning with the book *The Unseen Realm* (2015), Dr. Michael Heiser exposited such scriptures enough to satisfy any scholar. Reluctantly, he accepted there were other divinities. With that, he began finding the unseen realm in many other Bible passages. Psalm 82:1 was the can-opener for his insights.

> God stands in the congregation of the mighty;
> He judges among the gods.

Moses affirmed the multi-god understanding of the spirit world in Deuteronomy 10:17.

> For the LORD your God is God of gods and Lord of
> lords, the great God, mighty and awesome, who
> shows no partiality nor takes a bribe.

Miriam led the rescued Israelites in a song after the exodus. The LORD's competition with the gods of Egypt was clear. They knew the targets of God's plagues: the spirits of darkness who ruled Egypt.

> Who is like You, O LORD, among the gods? Who is
> like You, glorious in holiness, fearful in praises,
> doing wonders? (Exodus 15:1)

> For the Egyptians were burying all their firstborn,
> whom the LORD had killed among them. Also

on their gods the LORD had executed judgments.
(Numbers 33:4)

Moses' father-in-law Jethro was a Midianite. Even looking from outside, he recognized the competitive arena of divinities, and the triumph of I AM over them all.

> "Now I know that the LORD is greater than all the
> gods; for in the very thing in which they behaved
> proudly, He was above them." Then Jethro,
> Moses' father-in-law, took a burnt offering and
> other sacrifices to offer to God. (Exodus 18:11–
> 12)

BE LOYAL TO GOD

By recognizing that spirits competed with YHWH for nations, we understand the first commandment and its distinction from the second. The warning persists throughout the Law: *do not be disloyal to Me.*

> You shall have no other gods before Me. (Exodus
> 20:3)
> You shall not bow down to their gods, nor serve
> them, nor do according to their works; but you
> shall utterly overthrow them and completely
> break down their sacred pillars. (Exodus 23:24)
> You shall make no covenant with them, nor with
> their gods. (Exodus 23:32)

THEY WERE DISLOYAL

The prophets of the LORD continually warned His people about false gods. God identified idolatry as disloyalty and adultery, with dire consequences. His spokesmen spoke little about the other eight commandments.

God's prophetic judgments were about their disloyalty, far more than their imperfections or sins. The exile of Israel was punishment for disloyalty, their preference for the spirits of darkness over I AM WHO I AM.

The prophet Hosea portrayed their disloyalty with a costly prophetic marriage. Matching the words from God, Hosea married a prostitute. When she returned to her trade, he bought her off the auction block. Their marital drama enacted Israel's disloyalty to Yahweh, and the loyalty in His re-claiming them.

> For their mother has played the harlot;
> She who conceived them has behaved shamefully.
> For she said, 'I will go after my lovers,
> Who give me my bread and my water,
> My wool and my linen,
> My oil and my drink.'
> "Therefore, behold,
> I will hedge up your way with thorns,
> And wall her in,
> So that she cannot find her paths.
> She will chase her lovers,
> But not overtake them;
> Yes, she will seek them, but not find them.
> Then she will say,
> 'I will go and return to my first husband,
> For then it was better for me than now.'
> For she did not know
> That I gave her grain, new wine, and oil,
> And multiplied her silver and gold—
> Which they prepared for Baal.
> "Therefore I will return and take away

My grain in its time
And My new wine in its season,
And will take back My wool and My linen,
Given to cover her nakedness.
Now I will uncover her lewdness in the sight of her
    lovers,
And no one shall deliver her from My hand.
I will also cause all her mirth to cease,
Her feast days,
Her New Moons,
Her Sabbaths—
All her appointed feasts.
"And I will destroy her vines and her fig trees,
Of which she has said,
'These are my wages that my lovers have given me.'
So I will make them a forest,
And the beasts of the field shall eat them.
I will punish her
For the days of the Baals to which she burned
    incense.
She decked herself with her earrings and jewelry,
And went after her lovers;
But Me she forgot," says the LORD. (Hosea 2:5–13)

NOTHING HAS CHANGED

The nation-claiming by darkness is now done in secrecy. For most of history, the principality enjoyed prestige from the armies and religions of their assigned nations.

But in today's globally connected world, the spirits are more subtle. Avoiding the limelight, they secretly claim the nations, the mountains of culture, and the halls of government.

Since the birth of Jesus' Church, we have been pushing at hell's gates. The fallen angels of darkness have gone undercover. But they still require efficiency.

To rule the many, they must use the few. Nothing has changed. To succeed against God's image-creatures, the devil's kings must claim groups of people.

CHAPTER 8

THE NATIONS STILL RAGE

OUR PARADIGM DICTATES OUR VIEW OF THE SURROUNDING world. Crossing boundaries—political, economic, racial, or cultural —makes it visible.

One reputation of Americans abroad is arrogance. Our cultural individualism sees the world revolves around us, and our influence as good and superior.

Other nations often regard us as conceited and pushy. But within them are those who desire our individual freedom, the fruit of our Christian roots.

Individuals have the chance to prove themselves good or bad. Our American individualism prizes that, but also obscures the unseen arena of nation-claimers.

That was not true of the early church. In the prophecies of Psalm 2 and 149, they quickly recognized the unseen competition. I call the two Psalms bookends. The second psalm announces their rebellion; the other bookend tells about their binding.

JESUS REFUSED THE BYPASS

We examined satan's nation-gathering before Jesus in the wilderness. The lord of the unseen kings offered his dark grip to the incarnate LORD God Almighty.

> And the devil said to Him, "All this authority I will
> give You, and their glory; for this has been deliv-
> ered to me, and I give it to whomever I wish.
> (Luke 4:6)

What possible attraction did satan implant in that offer? After all, Jesus knew that the government of nations would be His.

> For unto us a Child is born,
> Unto us a Son is given;
> And the government will be upon His shoulder.
> And His name will be called
> Wonderful, Counselor, Mighty God,
> Everlasting Father, Prince of Peace.
> Of the increase of His government and peace
> There will be no end. (Isaiah 9:6–7)

But prophecy also told Jesus that three years' vexation and cruci-fixion for sin lay ahead.

> He is despised and rejected by men,
> A Man of sorrows and acquainted with grief.
> And we hid, as it were, our faces from Him;
> He was despised, and we did not esteem Him....
> But He was wounded for our transgressions,
> He was bruised for our iniquities;
> The chastisement for our peace was upon Him,
> And by His stripes we are healed.

All we like sheep have gone astray;
We have turned, every one, to his own way;
And the LORD has laid on Him the iniquity of us all.
    (Isaiah 53:3, 5–6)

Our highway bypass avoids the downtown, for a smooth drive around. The devil offered Jesus a smoother drive, even a shortcut to the lordship of nations. To claim them immediately, Jesus need only accept satan's offer.

Thank you, Jesus, for bravely refusing that bypass.

HISTORY'S BIGGEST BACKFIRE

When Jesus poured out the Holy Spirit on His Church, all hell broke loose. Now on earth were human beings like Adam and Eve, restored as living spirits, PLUS filled with God Himself. For satan and his partners, this created the highest threat level since losing heaven's war.

That escalation of the human race into the Church race explains Apostle Paul's shocking revelation of the backfire.

> But we speak the wisdom of God in a mystery, the
>   hidden wisdom which God ordained before the
>   ages for our glory, which none of the rulers of
>   this age knew; for had they known, they would
>   not have crucified the Lord of glory. (1
>   Corinthians 2:7–8)

With his pawns, the devil had orchestrated the humiliating crucifixion for God incarnate. But the dark happiness was short-lived. Jesus immediately raided satan's prison, impervious to any accuser's claim on His person. The lord of evil might salvage some pride, but two more humiliations awaited him. Jesus rose from the dead and poured His own Spirit into His followers.

In the end, Apostle Paul says satan regretted the crucifixion of Jesus. The net result was worse than before: human spirits were reborn, they would increase, and they were filled with God's own Spirit.

What could satan do after such a tremendous backfire? More of the same.

THE CLAIMERS THREATEN THE APOSTLES

The devil recognized that only eleven authorized disciples remained. So his religious puppets arrested them to silence them.

> Now as they spoke to the people, the priests, the
> captain of the temple, and the Sadducees came
> upon them, being greatly disturbed that they
> taught the people and preached in Jesus the
> resurrection from the dead. And they laid hands
> on them, and put them in custody until the
> next day, for it was already evening. (Acts 4:1–
> 3)

But this backfired as well. Before the Sanhedrin stood eleven new human spirits, with God's Spirit filling them—privileges the religious leaders refused to perceive.

Why would they discount the lame man's healing? To remain close-minded. After penalizing the eleven, they issued an empty threat to stop. Whatever murderous animosity there was, it became confused and powerless.

> What shall we do to these men? For, indeed, that a
> notable miracle has been done through them is
> evident to all who dwell in Jerusalem, and we
> cannot deny it. But so that it spreads no further
> among the people, let us severely threaten them,

that from now on they speak to no man in this name. (Acts 4:16–17)

THE CHURCH SEES THE CLAIMERS

The apostles' worldview identified satan's claimers in this event. They recognized it from the second Psalm. The thousands of new believers were all Jews who knew the psalm and prayed in unity using it.

> They raised their voice to God with one accord and
>> said: "Lord, You are God, who made heaven and
>> earth and the sea, and all that is in them, who by
>> the mouth of Your servant David have said:

>> 'Why did the nations rage,
>> And the people plot vain things?
>> The kings of the earth took their stand,
>> And the rulers were gathered together
>> Against the LORD and against His Christ.'
>> [quoting Psalm 2:1–2]

> "For truly against Your holy Servant Jesus, whom
>> You anointed, both Herod and Pontius Pilate,
>> with the Gentiles and the people of Israel, were
>> gathered together to do whatever Your hand and
>> Your purpose determined before to be done."
> (Acts 4:24–28)

This psalm told them what the warfare was. Apostle Paul would later summarize it in Ephesians 6:12 after penetrating many *ethnos*. The nations and their unseen claimers could not hide from the new Christians.

Psalms 2 and 149 had told them; both are cited in full below.

Both name the unseen kings that Jesus saw from the devil's high mountain (2:2, 149:8). The language-group nations are the competitive arena.

PSALM 2

1 Why do the nations rage,
And the people plot a vain thing?
2 The kings of the earth set themselves,
And the rulers take counsel together,
Against the LORD and against His Anointed, saying,
3 "Let us break Their bonds in pieces
And cast away Their cords from us."
4 He who sits in the heavens shall laugh;
The Lord shall hold them in derision.
5 Then He shall speak to them in His wrath,
And distress them in His deep displeasure:
6 "Yet I have set My King
On My holy hill of Zion."
7 "I will declare the decree:
The LORD has said to Me,
'You are My Son,
Today I have begotten You.
8 Ask of Me, and I will give You
The nations for Your inheritance,
And the ends of the earth for Your possession.
9 You shall break them with a rod of iron;
You shall dash them to pieces like a potter's vessel.' "
10 Now therefore, be wise, O kings;
Be instructed, you judges of the earth.
11 Serve the LORD with fear,
And rejoice with trembling.
12 Kiss the Son, lest He be angry,

And you perish in the way,
When His wrath is kindled but a little.
Blessed are all those who put their trust in Him.

When they rebelled in heaven, the fallen angels broke God's bonds and lordship over them. The time frame in Psalm 2 is the ongoing contest. The praying Church recognized that Jesus' persecution was the rage of the nation-dominators.

Jesus' trials manifested the continuing rebellion; so did the threats against the apostles and the new Church. Psalm 2 includes us who *kiss the Son* and trust Him.

Psalm 149 has the contrasting tone of praise, right before the rebellion is exhausted and its fallen angels bound. Psalm 149:5–9 includes us saints, the ones honored to bind these invisible enemies.

PSALM 149

1 Praise the LORD!
Sing to the LORD a new song,
And His praise in the assembly of saints.
2 Let Israel rejoice in their Maker;
Let the children of Zion be joyful in their King.
3 Let them praise His name with the dance;
Let them sing praises to Him with the timbrel and
    harp.
4 For the LORD takes pleasure in His people;
He will beautify the humble with salvation.
5 Let the saints be joyful in glory;
Let them sing aloud on their beds.
6 Let the high praises of God be in their mouth,
And a two-edged sword in their hand,
7 To execute vengeance on the nations,
And punishments on the peoples;

8 To bind their kings with chains,
And their nobles with fetters of iron;
9 To execute on them the written judgment—
This honor have all His saints.
Praise the LORD!

THE CHURCH BINDS THEM

The King's triumph includes delegation to His army of living human spirits. With His Word in our mouths—*the written judgment*—we execute His judgments on the kings and nobles, seen and unseen. We are God's army for vengeance on the claimers of the bookend psalms.

Apostle John beheld the triumphant King with His army of saints.

> Now I saw heaven opened, and behold, a white
> horse. And He who sat on him was called
> Faithful and True, and in righteousness He
> judges and makes war.... And the armies in
> heaven, clothed in fine linen, white and clean,
> followed Him on white horses. Now out of His
> mouth goes a sharp sword, that with it He
> should strike the nations. (Revelation 19:11, 14–
> 15)

JESUS AUTHORIZED US

By using the word *church* only three times, Jesus limited Himself to our key attributes as His Body. The first was to Peter, below, with an army mission delegated to us. Observe His language of bonds and binding, from Psalms 2 and 149.

> And I also say to you that you are Peter, and on this
> rock I will build My church, and the gates of

Hades shall not prevail against it. And I will give
you the keys of the kingdom of heaven, and
whatever you bind on earth will be bound in
heaven, and whatever you loose on earth will be
loosed in heaven. (Matthew 16:18–19)

He repeatedly expressed His intention to delegate the claimers'
judgment to us. One example was at the last supper, twelve hours
before His death to open the door for us. The second below was
prior to His ascension.

And I bestow upon you a kingdom, just as My Father
bestowed one upon Me. (Luke 22:29)

And Jesus came and spoke to them, saying, "All
authority has been given to Me in heaven and on
earth. Go therefore and make disciples of all the
nations." (Matthew 28:18–19)

Jesus' intention is at odds with our individualistic Christian
paradigm. If reality revolves around rights and opportunities, we
don't see the competition of unseen nation-rulers.

Then we can't represent the Judge, or bind enemy principalities.
Our effectiveness is nil in the contest of the unseen kings.

No wonder satan likes the nation-claiming system today. But
why did he like it in the first place?

CHAPTER 9

HOW NATION-CLAIMING HELPED THE DEVIL

LUCIFER WAS A CREATED BEING. THE MOST EXALTED AND ornamental, yes, but only a creature. He had limits in heaven. He did not know everything, could only be in one place at a time, and must trade to get what he wanted.

The same is true now. He rebelled and was cast down to Earth with the same limits. The fallen Lucifer is not the anti-god.

CREATOR'S PURPOSE

God and satan are not equals by any stretch of the imagination. It is His will that the kingdom of those evil creatures should exist for now. The only Creator entered the competition, but not for necessity. Both His justice and His love honor our human choice as the deciding factor.

It's temporary and has a purpose: to test us.

> The LORD your God led you all the way these forty
> years in the wilderness, to humble you and test
> you, to know what was in your heart, whether

you would keep His commandments or not.
(Deuteronomy 8:2)

The word of Jesus holds all things together, including the unseen tempters. They don't exist because they want to, any more than we do. They exist for their Creator's purpose, to perfect us.

> God, who at various times and in various ways spoke
> in time past to the fathers by the prophets, has in
> these last days spoken to us by His Son, whom
> He has appointed heir of all things, through
> whom also He made the worlds; who being the
> brightness of His glory and the express image of
> His person, and upholding all things by the word
> of His power, when He had by Himself purged
> our sins, sat down at the right hand of the
> Majesty on high. (Hebrews 1:1–3)

> For by Him all things were created that are in heaven
> and that are on earth, visible and invisible,
> whether thrones or dominions or principalities
> or powers. All things were created through Him
> and for Him. And He is before all things, and in
> Him all things consist. (Colossians 1:16–17)

MORE STABLE NUMBER

Claiming the *ethnos* was the devil's fourth strategy to regain dominion of Earth. He could control the *most* people with the *least* effort. Nation-claiming offered efficiency.

After the Flood, darkness faced a daunting prospect: humanity was multiplying. Absent the food competition from cursed ground, new leisure enabled our fertility. In contrast, satan and his fellow rebels cannot reproduce or reinforce themselves.

People were spreading over a much wider territory after Babel. Our combined spread and number would overtax infertile darkness, who are not everywhere like God. Most human beings would quickly be outside of their influence, if satan didn't come up with something quick.

God's division into *ethnos* gave opportunity for their evil. People-groups do not breed or multiply. The *ethnos* were a far more stable number, growing only slowly compared to the number of individual people.

By any measure, people-groups and their cultures are far more manageable for darkness. Culture has seven mountains, confirmed by prophetic revelation and sociological observation. Political nations numbered seventy-eight in 1900, and one-hundred-ninety-five today. Linguists estimate there are seven thousand language-groups. Ethnicities are only 24,000, using the strictest definition for each.

Compared to eight billion individuals, it's far easier for darkness to corrupt those small, stable numbers of groups. Snaring each group's few leaders and influencers, all people could fall prey to sin and alienation—both from God and from each other.

CHOKEPOINTS AND BOTTLENECKS

Strategies one through three targeted individual people, to corrupt their multiplication. The devil used each person as a chokepoint. By that person's disobedience to God, darkness infiltrated all succeeding generations. Cain's line exemplifies the infection of generations by satan's partner Sin.

But there were soon too many people for the limited number of fallen angels. Darkness can't make babies. The multiplication of God's image was the greatest threat to their rule on Earth.

The first three strategies each extended the chokepoint further into humanity. His fallen angel army was stretched to oppress individuals one-by-one. Hell's police-state control over the henchmen was at risk.

Targeting one or two people when there weren't many of us was a manageable bottleneck. But with each generation, it widened until it was no bottleneck at all. One-to-one tempting—first two, then four, and later the many daughters of men—required more partners for the devil.

Unless the kingdom of darkness could target humanity in subsets, every human birth would further overtax their ability to destroy.

God's language-creation at Babel made the job easier for the devil. Now he could assign his henchmen to a people-group. These bottlenecks made it easier to destroy righteousness among men, using fewer partners.

With the stable number of people-groups, satan's deputies could corrupt all people through their leaders and cultures. Needing fewer dark delegates, their ruthless prison-master could avoid dependence on partners.

Like any tyrant, the fewer he has to depend upon, the tighter his control. The prison of satan could retain its prisoners.

Is this the man who made the earth tremble,
Who shook kingdoms,
Who made the world as a wilderness
And destroyed its cities,
Who did not open the house of his prisoners?
(Isaiah 14:16–17)

He [Jesus] went and preached to the spirits in
    prison...
(1 Peter 3:20)

The *ethnos* strategy kept the partners closer to satan, where he can demote them or return them to imprisonment more easily. The fallen Lucifer brought the chokepoint backward into the kingdom of darkness. He strengthened himself as the chokepoint of all power in his kingdom.

REVEALED BEFORE JESUS

So much Christian speech treats the devil as an anti-god. It bears repeating: the fallen Lucifer can only be in one place at a time. Strategy four of nation-claiming required reliance on satan's partners. Their only previous collaboration was the intermarrying of strategy three (Genesis 6:1-5).

Consider who we Christians are. Only with the work of Jesus could people become born as living spirits. We live in that unseen realm, as do the hosts of heaven, both holy and unholy (Zechariah 3:7, Ephesians 2:6).

But the Old Testament prophets were not all privy to the unseen realm. In contrast to us, they received only situational glimpses. The *ethnos*-claiming strategy better explains their relevance to us. Through the prophets, God revealed darkness' grip on nation-chokepoints. Their writings name many people-groups.

Of course, the prophets did not encounter all Earth's people-groups, whether known or on the other six new continents. The ones not yet discovered they named as *the coastlands* and *beyond the Sea*.

BLACKMAIL POWER

The rulers of evil developed blackmail and incentive techniques. Blackmail controlled leaders when darkness could threaten to reveal their embarrassing secrets. Incentives secured allegiance from influential members of each *ethnos*.

With its IOU system, darkness propped up its preferred dictators and protected compliant influencers. It reduced entire regions, ethnicities, kingdoms, and language groups to pawns of satan.

We know from the prophetic judgments in the Old Testament, darkness succeeded. But knowing that is our motivation to identify, resist, and sever the unseen claims of darkness from our own *ethnos*— in our lives, our families, and our society.

One by one, the principalities claimed the people-groups. Footholds in the lives of a few influential people became strongholds in the entire nation, entwining all its people into sin. Kings became puppets, jerked around by the principalities that installed them.

The designated proxy could insinuate sins throughout the leaders of each people-group. That's why their kings typologically reveal the principality behind them; Ezekiel 28 and Tyre are one example.

SWEET REVENGE

The fallen rebels had suffered personally at the hands of God's holiness. Now they could use holiness against Him.

God intended His image-creatures to replace satan as Earth's dominators. But if people-groups became detestable to Him, satan's revenge would be sweet.

Once God claimed His own *ethnos*, the dark kingdom had an easier job. They only needed to make one people unholy: His own.

IOU POWER

Such a result would satisfy the unseen enemies. They burn with jealousy of us, knowing that mortals made of dirt are their replacements. No other creature was made in God's image.

To maintain their own power, they had to be *over* us so we wouldn't squeeze them out of dominion. That is the power pattern throughout darkness.

The devil dominates his subordinates tyrannically. Imagine he was your boss. Walking on eggshells, your fear would be demotion. Your nightmare would be returning to his prison of Isaiah 14:17.

That pattern of domineering control permeates darkness. With their assigned people-groups, the principalities copy his IOU system over the leaders of the *ethnos*.

The central question in the kingdom of darkness and its leadership structure isn't respect, nor fairness, nor success. It's this: Who wrote the IOUs, and who holds them now? Who has the leverage?

IOU TRADE

Trades based on IOUs create both winners and losers. The win-lose mindset among people copies Lucifer's trading in heaven, which caused his downfall.

God revealed the origin of satan to Ezekiel. The prince of the trading capital, Tyre, was the typological figure. Trading is one reason the exalted Lucifer fell.

> By the abundance of your trading
> You became filled with violence within,
> And you sinned. (Ezekiel 28:16)

LOVE TRADE

God loves trading. When only angels like Lucifer existed, there was trading.

In His kingdom, trades are always win-win. In Revelation 17–18, God's judgment on Babylon is trade-based. It reveals that holiness births trades of love, not IOUs.

The heaven awaiting us includes trading because He likes it.

> And the nations of those who are saved shall walk in
> its light, and the kings of the earth bring their
> glory and honor into it. Its gates shall not be shut
> at all by day (there shall be no night there). And
> they shall bring the glory and the honor of the
> nations into it. (Revelation 21:24–26)

Elsewhere in the *Unseen* Series

Book Three explores Ezekiel 27, naming fifty contracts of Tyre's merchants to show God's intimate concern for commercial trade.

ANGELS AND TRADING

When walking the fiery stones around heaven's throne, the archangel controlled angels' direct interaction with God. Five Bible passages reveal Lucifer's misuse of privilege. He leveraged his exclusive position with IOU trading. Angels who wanted to interact with God had to give Lucifer an open-ended obligation.

God uniquely equipped the angelic hosts to discern honor. The One they disdained measured their consequence when they prized pleasing Lucifer more greatly. That's why they cannot repent.

But between God and angels, the scripture reveals no intimacy. It reserves relationships for God and the creature in His image.

> For indeed He does not give aid to angels, but He
> does give aid to the seed of Abraham. (Hebrews
> 2:16)

UNREAL IOUs

Wherever God is, is true reality. Lucifer's position was the most exalted of any creature: walking the fiery pavement which originally surrounded God's throne. What could any angel could offer in trade to one with that privilege?

> You were the anointed cherub who covers;
> I established you;

You were on the holy mountain of God;
You walked back and forth in the midst of fiery
    stones.
(Ezekiel 28:24-14)

But Lucifer was unsatisfied by his created privilege and went away to trading posts throughout the angelic population.

You defiled your sanctuaries
By the multitude of your iniquities,
By the iniquity of your trading...
(Ezekiel 28:18)

When I AM, who is reality itself, is unwelcomed or dishonored, falsity appears real. The archangel forsook the honor of God's presence and immediately began falling for the delusional idea he could replace God.

For you have said in your heart:
'I will ascend into heaven,
I will exalt my throne above the stars of God;
I will also sit on the mount of the congregation
On the farthest sides of the north;
I will ascend above the heights of the clouds,
I will be like the Most High.'
(Isaiah 14:13–14)

Angels who traded with Lucifer—for no other creatures existed then—also fell under a delusion. In a false magnanimity, the deceptive Lucifer could let them pass, for a *something to be determined later.*

That *something* was help with his rebellion against God. Revelation 12 suggests that a third of the angels joined his rebellion. Those partner-rebels didn't have the same deluded ambition he had, to replace God. Why did they join Lucifer then?

I believe it was to fulfill their IOUs to Lucifer.

CHAPTER 10

THE FRAGILITY OF SATAN

THE SUBORDINATES OF SATAN WERE NOT HAPPY ABOUT their fate; instead, they harbored resentment of his oppression. God revealed this through Isaiah, using the future king of Babylon as a type of Lucifer.

> Those who see you will gaze at you,
> And consider you, saying:
> 'Is this the man who made the earth tremble,
> Who shook kingdoms,
> Who made the world as a wilderness
> And destroyed its cities,
> Who did not open the house of his prisoners?
> (Isaiah 14:16-17)

Tricked by their IOUs to him, they joined his rebellion out of obligation. As angels they had no repentance; their eternity was to burn within under his brutal, jealous thumb.

Such an oppressive system of authority and power caused

internal resentments. With no love and only ambition, division is the predicted result.

Recognizing this makes sense of Bible revelation about the kingdom of darkness. Jesus read it in the scriptures. That's how He knew about its internal doom—from division.

> Every kingdom divided against itself is brought to
> desolation, and a house divided against a house
> falls. If satan also is divided against himself, how
> will his kingdom stand? (Luke 11:17–18)

THE LOGIC OF PRINCIPALITIES

No fallen angel could escape satan's heartless rule. They could not rebel against him as he had against God. The archangel is impervious to anything his entire corp of partners might try. The fallen angels are more afraid of him than any human they oppress. Scripture records no attempt to replace satan; they never organize against him.

The tyranny of leveraged IOUs descended through the ranks of darkness' rigid hierarchy.

As Seen Yesterday, Today & Tomorrow

Human history amply demonstrates that such ambition always results in the oppression of others, and this history has its origin in darkness.

The fallen angels had a choice. One option was eternal torment in the prison of a crazed satan with an angelic supremacy matched by his depraved hostility. The preferable option two would be to oppress people under his direction. Each partner-rebel could become a principality over nations, a limited divinity of their own, if they were compliant.

Their only relief from satan's oppression was for them to oppress people as many as possible. "I will lose to satan, no matter what I try. So I will oppress everyone else and get brownie points with him."

Lucifer's original nature of greatness, intelligence, and power, formerly devoted to God's service, now qualified him to be the undisputed leader of rebel angels.

THE DEPENDENCY OF SATAN

The devil wants to oppress as many as possible. To keep spirits in his prison, the dark leader wants the minimum number of partners needed to ruin humanity.

If he hadn't needed partners, satan would not release them from his prison. *He did not open the house of his prisoners.* (Isaiah 14:17) But he did need them, to defeat the rapidly multiplying image-creatures of God.

And therein lies the fragility of satan: he is dependent upon partners. It includes his dependence upon people. If no one cooperated with his schemes, the millennial reign of Jesus might have started long ago. But we are all born dead in spirit, and are raw meat for the kingdom of darkness. His partner Sin (strategy two) has done a good job for him.

IMPLEMENTATION OF IOUs

The failure of the first three strategies forced satan to use more partners. He released some fallen angels from his prison. But the fallen satan must relentlessly dominate his subordinates.

He keeps them in thrall with his system of IOUs, promising rewards and threatening punishments. He had a protection racket, like any self-respecting mobster would.

In exchange for their functional freedom, satan gave them responsibility to ruin the *ethnos* under the nation-claiming strategy. Their freedom was organized, restricted, and conditional. Compliance and success were required to fulfill their IOU, or their parole would be revoked.

As Seen Today

With the movies and the fiction of our civilization, we've seen such confabs of mobsters and wicked people—their fake compliments, their bravado, their begrudging manipulation of one another, their divvying up the spoils, their assigning to one another the wickedness to perform.

In Luke 11, Jesus reveals that the kingdom of darkness is divided and will fall (contrary to Lincoln's application of the verse during the American Civil War history). Not surprisingly, that's what our fiction about bad guys almost always displays: mobsters always turn on one another.

The freedom that darkness promises us is always false. The walls of consequence close in relentlessly when we choose to agree with satan instead of God Almighty.

CHOKEPOINTS MEAN FEWER PAROLEES

The devil wanted to release the fewest partners possible. Controlling the *ethnos* with a few paroled principalities was an economical use of "manpower" for satan. Chokepoints made it possible. Meanwhile, unneeded partners could be kept in his prison.

The repopulation of humanity was flourishing at Babel and threatened to outstrip the number of satan and his partners in darkness. But division into a small number of language-groups helped darkness. Through principalities over each group, satan could compete for domination of Earth.

Bottlenecks and chokepoints are efficient. The dark warden paroles the minimum number needed to manage these points of control. With their IOU system over human leaders, the partners rule their assigned *ethnos*.

INTERNAL AFFAIRS

As the saying goes, *if they will do it with you, they will do it to you.* These fallen angels had rebelled with Lucifer and far outnumbered him. Now resentful for the mess he got them into, what would keep them from rebelling against him?

The devil must maintain his preeminence as king of darkness. He leverages his fallen partners against one another so they will not contest him. Ideally, he can incite such hate among them, they always fight each other and never him. As Jesus said: divided.

ROTATING RULERS

Armies rotate commanders among units. It prevents any one commander from becoming a mutinous threat to the command structure. The devil also rotates his principalities and the periods of their power. None can gain power to mutiny or challenge his choke-hold on power.

No prophet of the Old Testament perceived this so clearly as Daniel. Nebuchadnezzar, Belshazzar, Cyrus, and Darius are the portrayal of empire-shuffling. The rotation of rulers dominates dreams. Archangel Gabriel reveals it plainly to Daniel in chapters 10–11.

Daniel held a prominent position in the courts of Babylon. From it, he witnessed the upheaval of nations and empires. When Gabriel described the unseen manipulation of nations, Daniel was an under-standing listener.

People-groups manifest the perpetual upheaval among principalities. Each nation-claimer has a promotion as its *ethnos* rises, and a demotion as it fades. The rotation of dark rulers explains why the nations of Earth have always risen and fallen.

GOD ENTERS THE FRAY

God divided and dispersed humanity at Babel. He explained why: because nothing would be impossible for us otherwise. But was it a backfire for the LORD? The new people-groups enabled the nation-claiming strategy. What would justify giving satan such opportunity for efficiency?

The first three strategies of darkness had failed to ruin all humanity. We were multiplying beyond what satan could handle. Why would God set up the fallen Lucifer with anything that would work for darkness?

I'm aware of no traditional theology which satisfies these questions.

Judging from the results, God's plan was to create a competition and enter it Himself. Nation-claiming makes sense of the entire Bible, beginning with Abraham's call. By claiming the descendants of Jacob as His people, God entered the arena with the dark claimers. The fallen angels whom He had created and exiled witnessed a personal engagement from Him which they had never seen before.

A MUCH DIFFERENT METHOD

Every *ethnos* has distinguishing characteristics. Each ruling spirit imposed unique qualities upon its claimed group. The murderous principalities replicated satan's IOUs and wickedness.

In contrast, Yahweh imposed distinctions upon Israel which expressed His holiness. His claimed people could honor Him with loyalty. God's distinctions for Israel were also beneficial for human fulfillment.

God's requirements were far more desirable. Why wouldn't everyone want the benefits God offered? How did the unseen claimers ensnare people to embrace distinctions of destruction?

One power-move they use is sorcery.

CHAPTER 11

THE SORCERERS OF THE CLAIMERS

THE FORCES OF EVIL THAT APOSTLE PAUL DESCRIBED IN Ephesians 6:12 throw their net widely. The more people they can influence into iniquitous patterns, the better. Their standard is low; only one habit of sin corrupts the entire people-group.

But God's claiming is unique among the *ethnos*-claims. God does not limit His requirements to behaviors, whether one or many.

Our God is restoring righteousness on Earth, as we overheard in Genesis 18 earlier. He does it with human partners to His kingdom, whom He trusts and who choose His narrow way. Such people synchronize with His desires, but there are few of us, as Jesus described.

> Enter by the narrow gate; for wide is the gate and
> broad is the way that leads to destruction, and
> there are many who go in by it. Because narrow is
> the gate and difficult is the way which leads to
> life, and there are few who find it. (Matthew
> 7:13–14)

SORCERERS

A dark method to claim dominance over nations was sorcery. Every nation's king had sorcerers who bastardized true spiritual reality apart from the true God. The corps of advisors included soothsayers, enchanters, and magicians.

Josiah was the last righteous king over Judah. He outlawed sorcerers in 2 Kings 23:24.

The kingdom of darkness planted them to give destructive advice to the visible rulers. Their influence was significant in the halls of kings. For one thing, the king decreed who the people's god would be. "Baal is our god," or "Chemosh is our god."

This inner circle further ensnared the entire nation into worship of their angelic divinities, making the *ethnos* detestable to God. Through the leading advisors, darkness extended their influence throughout the fabric of a nation.

The Counterfeit & the Real

Royal advisors had to qualify for royal trust. With their connection to darkness, they received enough accuracy from the principality to establish their credibility.

Even counterfeiters require credibility by being useful. These ambassadors of satan mimic the prophetic accuracy of God's people. It is us Christians, filled with the Holy Spirit, who can speak His word in any situation.

The unseen force of these advisors would be hard to detect, or even irresistible. In the Bible, pagan rulers often required dreams to hear the true God, sleep being one time outside the sorcerers' influence.

Pharaoh's advising magicians duplicated the first three signs Moses and Aaron did. Study of the passage shows Pharaoh's reliance on them. The advisors functioned as gatekeepers against outside persuasion. These magicians and witches could endorse or condemn people before Pharaoh.

The principality over Egypt thus embedded its hidden influences into Egyptian culture and governance. But this wasn't new at the time of Moses and Aaron. The dark infiltration was present four centuries earlier, with Joseph.

SORCERY AND JOSEPH

Unjustly imprisoned and forgotten, Jacob's son Joseph was in an Egyptian dungeon when Pharaoh had two dreams which seem plain enough to us: "famine is coming."

In the Bible record, the sorcerers *could not* interpret them (Genesis 41:8). In our actual experience, we understand it to mean *would not*. No advisor wants to be the bearers of such bad tidings to Pharaoh. Advisors who risk unwelcome advice to a king are elusive in every court.

Joseph interpreted the two dreams, and Pharaoh raised him to a stature above the magical advisors. But their influence was empowered by unseen rulers, and Joseph adopted their practice of divination with a silver cup dedicated for it—the same cup he put in Benjamin's grain sack. We hear this from Joseph's own mouth.

> Is not this the one from which my lord drinks, and
>   with which he indeed practices divina-
>   tion?... Joseph said to them, "What deed is this
>   you have done? Did you not know that such a
>   man as I can certainly practice divination?" (Gen-
>   esis 44:5, 15)

From Joseph to Moses was four centuries. The sorcerers of the two Pharaohs were deeply rooted in Egyptian society. Their credibility was well-established ahead of Joseph's time.

SORCERY AND MOSES

The top graduates of Pharaoh's magic school turned their rods into a snake, duplicating the sign that God gave Moses. They also turned water into blood and created frogs out of water, just as Moses and Aaron had done at God's own command.

The Bible acknowledges sorcery as an actual power, implementing an accurate spiritual knowledge. Why would the Holy Spirit inspire the record of sorcery as real?

It's further warning for us; we must not discount the genuine power of the unholy. Subject to limits, the kingdom of darkness can create, accelerate, and reshape. They can even counterfeit qualities of God's work. The representatives of satan can be accurate, but they are never true.

Elsewhere in the *Unseen* Series

Book Three's study of Genesis 1:2 revealed physical capabilities for the fallen. The exiled Lucifer and his partners reshaped the original Earth into a dark and watery cooling pool, formless and void.

The Bible doesn't dismiss witchcraft as fiction. If we do, it provides power to their deception. Sorcery is a real power, and relies upon a real knowledge.

Egypt's influential sorcerers were not alone. Groups of magicians feature repeatedly.

SORCERY AND SAUL

King Saul spared an enemy king at his own prerogative while self-delusional that he had obeyed God. But the judge and prophet Samuel saw through it. Yahweh clearly instructed Saul to kill every Amalekite (1 Samuel 15:3).

Samuel's assessment shows acute recognition of witchcraft and sorcery. He lumped Saul with the magicians and idolaters so common in kings' courts.

Behold, to obey is better than sacrifice,
And to heed than the fat of rams.
For rebellion is as the sin of witchcraft,
And stubbornness is as iniquity and idolatry.
(1 Samuel 15:22–23)

Saul excused his disobedience as ninety-nine percent faithful to God's command. Outwardly compliant, Saul nurtured hypocrisy within—and didn't even recognize it.

Prophet Samuel was Saul's only spiritual guide. When the prophet died, Saul outlawed all spiritists including witches (1 Samuel 28:3). Yet, as his reign neared its end and his death approached, the king was desperate. In disguise, Saul visited the witch of En Dor, who specialized in summoning the dead.

She is yet another witness to the reality of sorcery. The witch of En Dor really raised Samuel's spirit from Sheol and communicated with him (1 Samuel 28:12–15), which defeated Saul's disguise. The Bible described the witch of En Dor as a real sorcerer with real power.

SORCERY AND ELIJAH

Scripture describes sorcery again in 1 Kings 18 on Mt. Carmel. The eight-hundred-fifty prophets of Baal and Ashtoreth suffered defeat and humiliation at Elijah's hand and paid with their lives.

They used sorcery to cajole a response from the unseen ruler called Baal. Darkness' unseen spirits are always moisture-seeking rulers; blood is always their craving. Magicians have used blood-drawing throughout history and in our day.

> "O Baal, hear us!"... Then they leaped about the altar
> which they had made.... So they cried aloud, and
> cut themselves, as was their custom, with knives
> and lances, until the blood gushed out on them.
> (1 Kings 18:26, 28)

One man alone, with a simple calm prayer, accomplished what hundreds could not. Imagine how humiliating their disaster was. Elijah did some cajoling too, but it wasn't toward God.

> Elijah mocked them and said, "Cry aloud, for he is a
> god; either he is meditating, or he is busy, or he is
> on a journey, or perhaps he is sleeping and must
> be awakened." (1 Kings 18:27)

SORCERY IN BABYLON

About six hundred years after the exodus from Egypt, Babylon conquered and deported the disloyal Jews. Among the exiles were teenagers Daniel and his three friends. In keeping with his royal policy, the king instructed they be given a proper education to serve his court.

> ...young men in whom there was no blemish, but
> good-looking, gifted in all wisdom, possessing
> knowledge and quick to understand, who had
> ability to serve in the king's palace, and whom
> they might teach the language and literature of
> the Chaldeans. (Daniel 1:4)

Daniel and his friends refused the wine and nutrition, but not the learning, the culture, and the language. The king of Babylon found that they excelled, and they submitted to him.

Why did they draw the line at the food, but not the knowledge? After all, Babylon's knowledge and culture made it a center of sorcery. Centuries later, God used Babylon as the poster child for sorcery: *for by your sorcery all the nations were deceived* (Revelation 18:23).

NEBUCHADNEZZAR'S DRAMA

God Himself had summoned Babylon's King Nebuchadnezzar to execute His judgment on nations (Jeremiah 25:9, Daniel 1:2). The sovereignty of God overrides all earthly rulers.

> It is He who sits above the circle of the earth,
> And its inhabitants are like grasshoppers,
> Who stretches out the heavens like a curtain,
> And spreads them out like a tent to dwell in. (Isaiah
>   40:22)

The magicians of darkness were prominent advisors in his court. But not all was well. Nebuchadnezzar's first dream arouses suspicion that his counselors are only yes-men. The decisive executive dramatically threatens them.

> If you do not make known the dream to me, and its
>   interpretation, you shall be cut in pieces, and
>   your houses shall be made an ash heap. (Daniel
>   2:5)

The king's skepticism about his magicians' self-serving motives opens the door for Daniel and his three friends. On the coattails of Daniel's accuracy, the sorcerers continued to surround Nebuchadnezzar. Despite his original suspicions of the sorcerers, he kept asking their interpretations.

But humiliation by the four exiles made the sorcerers his sworn enemies. This group was a primary weapon of the principality against anyone from God's *ethnos*. When the three friends refused to bow to Nebuchadnezzar's golden statue, advisors were the tattle-tale group (Daniel 3:8-12). Despite the beatdowns the magician corps kept receiving, their influence continued.

SORCERY AND BABYLON'S FALL

The implanted sorcerers represented the principality of Babylon throughout the reign of Nebuchadnezzar and right to the end of the empire. His son Belshazzar inherited the crew of darkness, and, as usual, they get the first call about the handwriting on the wall.

> The king cried aloud to bring in the astrologers, the
> Chaldeans, and the soothsayers. The king spoke,
> saying to the wise men of Babylon, "Whoever
> reads this writing, and tells me its interpretation,
> shall be clothed with purple and have a chain of
> gold around his neck; and he shall be the third
> ruler in the kingdom." Now all the king's wise
> men came, but they could not read the writing,
> or make known to the king its interpretation.
> (Daniel 5:7–8)

Evidently, their schooling prohibited confirming bad news to a king. He knew it wasn't good and couldn't stand unassisted. After all, it was three simple words in a known language: numbered, weighed, wanting.

Daniel had been the only fall-back interpreter in Babylon for decades, yet completely forgotten until the queen brought him up.

All the magicians sheltered under Babylon's wing found out he was accurate, yet again.

They had to find a new patron the following day. The Medes and Persians under Cyrus were marching in through the flood gates, even as Belshazzar banqueted.

Just as the nation-claiming system persists to our own day, so does witchcraft. The sorcery schools continued into the New Testament time, both in Jesus' ministry and in the early church.

CHAPTER 12

SORCERY IN THE NEW TESTAMENT

THE NEW TESTAMENT EXPLICITLY RECORDS THE PRACTICE of sorcery. Jesus Himself was accused of sorcery by Jewish critics. His retort is equally telling, focusing on their own methods.

> But some of them said, "He casts out demons by
> Beelzebub, the ruler of the demons." (Luke
> 11:15)

> And if I cast out demons by Beelzebub, by whom do
> your sons cast them out? Therefore they will be
> your judges. (11:19)

SORCERY AND SIMON

The apostles' vigilance against witchcraft appears in Acts 8, which describes the deacon Philip's evangelism in Samaria. One new convert attempted to keep his sorcery. Apostle Peter and John gave harsh rebuke and exclusion to the sorcerer, Simon of Samaria.

> Now for some time a man named Simon had prac-
> ticed sorcery in the city and amazed all the people
> of Samaria. He boasted that he was someone
> great, and all the people, both high and low, gave
> him their attention and exclaimed, "This man is
> rightly called the Great Power of God." They
> followed him because he had amazed them for a
> long time with his sorcery. (Acts 8:9-24)

Simon was a prominent Samaritan influence because of his sorcery. But the people believed Philip's gospel and rejoiced in the subsequent miracles. Simon did what everyone was doing. He became a Christian and was baptized in the name of Jesus.

But Simon had not become a true disciple. He saw the miracles as a way to protect his influence. Apostles Peter and John came to affirm Philip's ministry and impart the Holy Spirit. That's when Simon unintentionally revealed his bad spiritual paradigm.

> When Simon saw that the Spirit was given at the
> laying on of the apostles' hands, he offered them
> money and said, "Give me also this ability so that
> everyone on whom I lay my hands may receive
> the Holy Spirit." (Acts 8:18–19)

Simon had believed the gospel and was baptized into the name of Jesus. Was that not all that was required? Although some Christian preaching says so, it was not. He was using God, not yielding to Him.

That's why Simon considered the Holy Spirit something to be bought—the Holy Spirit of God Himself. How did he get this wicked, ludicrous idea? From the normal ways power was bought. Simon's reputation was built on sorcery bought with money. His motive as a new Christian was the same as before: to be a prominent influencer.

How do you know if someone is saved? After all, Simon had

believed and been baptized in water. But for his entire life, darkness had seduced him. Oppression easily blinds anyone to the holiness of God's Spirit. Discipleship must follow salvation and baptism; growth is required so we can shed the blindfolds we never recognized before.

Peter immediately rebukes Simon.

> Peter answered: "May your money perish with you, because you thought you could buy the gift of God with money! You have no part or share in this ministry, because your heart is not right before God. Repent of this wickedness and pray to the Lord in the hope that he may forgive you for having such a thought in your heart. For I see that you are full of bitterness and captive to sin." (Acts 8:20–23)

Moderns might regard Peter's rebuke as harsh or intolerant. But love for the new convert is the apostle's motive. He permits Simon no confusion about his actual spiritual condition.

Peter had heard Jesus' warnings that spiritual power was no guarantee of salvation (Matthew 7:22–23). His rebuke protected Simon from a false salvation and closed the door on sorcery in the Church.

There's only one remedy for oppression by darkness. We must be filled with the opposite spirit: the Holy Spirit. Otherwise, the convert suddenly swept clean—such as Simon—falls prey to the same demon plus seven worse. Peter implements Jesus' warning in his rebuke to Simon.

And when he comes, he finds it swept and put in order. Then he goes and takes with him seven other spirits more wicked than himself, and they enter and dwell there; and the last state of that man is worse than the first. (Luke 11:24–26)

SORCERY AND CAIN

Peter told Simon he was still a captive to sin. That's what God had warned Cain about.

> So the Lord said to Cain, "Why are you angry? And
> why has your countenance fallen? If you do well,
> will you not be accepted? And if you do not do
> well, sin lies at the door. And its desire is for
> you, but you should rule over it." (Genesis 4:6–
> 7)

Like Cain, Simon of Samaria wanted God's favor. But Peter saw his bitterness over being deposed as an influencer. Sin captivated Simon, as it had Cain. The ungodly belief for both men was that God could be bought.

Cain thought he could manipulate God's favor on his own terms, the substandard sacrifice. Simon of Samaria thought he could manipulate God with money, treating the *Holy* Spirit as a common spirit.

Obvious to Simon, money is required to gain such great power; he had paid money for his sorcery scrolls and the powers he learned. Simon couldn't see any difference. Peter and John recognized Simon was perilously close to the unforgivable sin.

> To him who blasphemes against the Holy Spirit, it
> will not be forgiven.(Luke 12:10)

Peter spoke to Simon's heart, and exhorted him to repent. He identified how the Holy Spirit was different. Simon wanted to lay hands on Christians, but the apostles excluded Simon from any ministry at all. It appears Simon took Peter's admonition seriously.

Then Simon answered, "Pray to the Lord for me so
that nothing you have said may happen to me."

Notice Simon's fear: *nothing you have said,* including the
perishing of his money and exclusion from ministry. Thus the record
leaves us uncertain whether Simon renounced his base motivations.

PAUL BLINDS ELYMAS

Paul's first stop in his first missionary journey included combat with
the kingdom of darkness, in Acts 13:8-11.

> But Elymas the sorcerer (for that is what his name
> means) opposed them and tried to turn the
> proconsul from the faith. Then Saul, who was
> also called Paul, filled with the Holy Spir-
> it, looked straight at Elymas and said, "You are a
> child of the devil and an enemy of everything
> that is right! You are full of all kinds of deceit and
> trickery. Will you never stop perverting the right
> ways of the Lord? Now the hand of the Lord is
> against you. You are going to be blind for a time,
> not even able to see the light of the sun." Imme-
> diately mist and darkness came over him, and he
> groped about, seeking someone to lead him by
> the hand.

Before he preached to the proconsul, Paul dealt with the sorcerer
using the same words Jesus used for his fellow Jews: *You are a child of
the devil* (Matthew 23:13-15, John 8:44). Those words reveal how
Paul identified sorcery, and the transformation he had undergone.

After Paul's conversion, Jesus trained him for fourteen years in
Arabia. The Lord would sharply refine Paul's perception of the
devil's schemes. No longer would the apostle see his fellow Pharisees

as the power circle. He would agree with Jesus that they were the devil's children. Paul spoke that way when they put him on trial.

Through reflection on his experiences among the religious leaders, Paul began recognizing spiritual forces of evil. Experiences had taught him how to wrestle unseen rulers, who used sorcerers to work their secretive influence.

At every biblical appearance of sorcerers like Simon and Elymas, we see God rapidly and summarily taking them down. The apostles got the message and spared no effort to root out sorcery.

Luke didn't record Elymas' ultimate response to the gospel. He had chosen darkness and gets more of it: blinding. God's judgment gives us more of what we want.

SORCERY IN THE EPHESIAN CHURCH

Seven sons of the itinerant Jewish exorcist Sceva came to Ephesus. They attempted to counterfeit Paul's deliverance ministry. Luke records their beat-down by a demon. A region-wide repentance for sorcery followed, in Acts 19:13-19.

> When this became known to the Jews and Greeks
> living in Ephesus, they were all seized with
> fear, and the name of the Lord Jesus was held in
> high honor. Many of those who believed now
> came and openly confessed what they had
> done. A number who had practiced sorcery
> brought their scrolls together and burned them
> publicly. When they calculated the value of the
> scrolls, the total came to fifty thousand
> drachmas.

Many of those who believed were still practicing sorcery, learned in part from their scrolls at home. They were not cheap, as the passage says. People treasured scrolls as heirlooms, containing the knowledge of past ages. Each scroll required many man-hours of copying, similar to ancient Bible scrolls.

Luke reports the value of these scrolls. Why would they have known each scroll's value, and tally them? Because there was a money investment and a current market value. That's no surprise, since sorcery conjures up actual powers of darkness. It's like Simon's sin, paying for spiritual power.

God quickly defeated sorcerers reported in Scripture. Likewise in Ephesus, He exposes them in the infancy of the local church. Jesus' parable says tares can grow alongside the wheat (Matthew 13:24-30), but sorcery is never one of them in Scripture.

SECRET DISLOYALTY

The Ephesian believers reveal that their salvation was half-hearted. Their original plan had been to continue sorcery in new Christian clothing. After all, sorcery was an accepted retail practice.

Withholding their scrolls has only one explanation: the new Christians were unwilling to give up sorcery. Whether planned and willfully hidden, or because of immaturity, their discipleship was not sincere until they renounced sorcery.

Our society regards Ouija boards and magic eight-balls as harmless fun. But the demonic beat-down brought home the reality of darkness. Only the public humiliation of Sceva's seven sorcerer sons pierced the hearts of the half-hearted Christians.

PUBLIC RENUNCIATION

The believers publicly demonstrated their discipleship intensity. They did not burn only scrolls. They burned the bridges to their past and their community.

These Christians did not consider the sorcery scrolls false, or would have thrown them away. The public disavowal shows the realization that sorcery was dangerously real. Their concern was not only themselves, but also their fellow Ephesians.

Publicly destroying the scrolls by fire and valuing them shows the addictive seriousness of sorcery. Open renunciation of their contents was hardly justified if they were useless. Quite the contrary: these scrolls had to be destroyed to keep them out of anyone else's hands, ever.

FIRE FOR DARKNESS

Ephesus was not the only burning. Mere decades after Jesus' ascension, one of the most costly fires ever occurred in the library of Alexandria, in Egypt. About 400,000 scrolls were reduced to ashes.

Naturally, they would include many topics. Just as in Ephesus, many would contain valuable sorcerers' knowledge. It's a preview of the final end of darkness, which God ends with fire.

> The devil, who deceived them, was cast into the lake
> of fire and brimstone where the beast and the
> false prophet are. And they will be tormented day
> and night forever and ever. (Revelation 20:10)

We've seen God's alacrity to root out all sorcery from His newborn Church. God permitted the library's destruction for the same reason that the Ephesians burned their scrolls.

What if magicians like Simon had brought such knowledge in? No wonder Apostle John admonishes us to test the spirits (1 John 4:1).

SORCERY SUPPORTS THE UNSEEN CLAIMERS

These practitioners of sorcery were the wise men of regions and kingdoms. Kings relied on their guidance. Through their recommendations, a principality would cement its claim on the nation assigned to it by satan.

To exterminate righteousness, the inner circle persuades kings to enact unjust laws. An example is Darius' decree about the lion's den. It promoted the divinity of the king. That's why Daniel was penalized for praying to YHWH.

The sorcerers installed dishonor for the only true God as a virtue in a nation. The nation became detestable to God and liable to His judgment—exactly what the kingdom of darkness wanted.

AN ALTERNATIVE

The principalities skillfully disguise their malevolence. Witchcraft and sorcery ensnare people and ethnic groups, leaving no escape. But what if there could be a relationship with a worthy spirit, that didn't abuse people with his power?

PART THREE

GOD CLAIMS HIS ETHNOS

The devil's dark princes claim entire nations and cultures, but they aren't the only ones who do it. God also claimed a nation for Himself. When He began lifting the curtain on the unseen, it was through the Jews.

We have the Word of God available to people of every tribe, language, and nation, because the claimed nation of God received it faithfully.

> What advantage then has the Jew, or what is the
> profit of circumcision? Much in every way!
> Chiefly because to them were committed the
> oracles of God. (Romans 3:1–2)

CHAPTER 13

GOD COMPETES

THE KINGDOM OF DARKNESS MAY HAVE REJOICED WHEN God divided humanity into *ethnos*. Nation-claiming was only possible because of people divided by language (and with time, cultural and family distinctions as well).

But did they realize it also opened an opportunity for God Himself? Not only satan, but God also interacts with humanity in groups. Choosing *ethnos* nations was He did as well. Yahweh staked His claim on just one people-group through Abram and Sarai.

GOD CALLS ABRAM

The LORD's call to Abram of Ur reveals His plan to bless all people.

> I will bless you
> And make your name great;
> And you shall be a blessing.
> I will bless those who bless you,
> And I will curse him who curses you;

And in you all the families of the earth shall be
blessed. (Genesis 12:2–3)

Imagine the dread when darkness overheard this. Were they surprised that God might claim a family? Possibly, satan's power-hungry self-esteem obscured any *loving* thing God might do.

Claiming a family might have been tolerable, except what God planned to do with it. He would bless all the nations of the earth. Not even the *ethnos* claimed by satan's henchmen were safe. Even the language groups corrupted, accused, and blackmailed by spiritual forces of wickedness? None were immune from God's plan.

Abraham's life events all dovetail with the nation-claiming system. God's claim on Isaac's line bore a message throughout the host of heaven. Not every *ethnos* would be claimed by these principalities.

Claiming an *ethnos* of His own, Yahweh would penetrate every *ethnos* with blessing.

ONE CLAIMED LINE

To the childless old Abraham and his aged wife Sarah, the LORD repeatedly promised great fruitfulness. The majority of God's recorded speech to them concerned their offspring and land.

Isaac was born to Sarah decades after her menopause, at Abraham's age 100. No other of Abraham's sons were in the line God claimed. Jacob is singled out rather than Esau.

Jesus was born to that lineage. When you were saved by faith in Him, God adopted you into that blessed line.

...you received the Spirit of adoption by whom we cry
out, "Abba, Father." (Romans 8:15)

VERSUS ANTI-SEMITISM

God sent His Word and His Son Jesus to all the world through Jews, His people-group. The Church does not replace the Jews as God's claimed *ethnos*.

Anti-Semitism is contrary to His claim, and disdains the exclusive privilege He reserves for them. Not all Jews follow Jesus, squandering their prized privilege. Yet as a people-group, they remain God's claim.

Apostle Paul understood. His first ministry in every location was to his fellow Jews. Only afterward did he preach to everyone else (*Gentiles*). Saved non-Jews are not superior; unbelieving Jews have no less opportunity until they die.

> If you were cut out of the olive tree which is wild by
> nature, and were grafted contrary to nature into a
> cultivated olive tree, how much more will these,
> who are natural branches, be grafted into their
> own olive tree? (Romans 11:24)

SHOCKING NEW DEVELOPMENT

Abraham's life events are well-known to us. But to enemies in the unseen realms, it was shocking and new. When they heard God call Abraham, it was dreadful, first-time news.

Ever since Babel, they had monopolized the nation-claiming marketplace. Never before had God entered the fray with satan and his cohorts, not even when the war in heaven occurred (Revelation 12). God had never claimed any being at all, not even angels.

They soon learned He was doing much more than claiming.

GOD INITIATES COVENANT

The covenant between YHWH and Abram developed from Genesis

chapters 15 to 17. Covenants were important in ancient society. Today we have many roughly equivalent words.

- contract
- agreement
- memorandum of understanding
- treaty
- articles of incorporation
- constitution

One difference between then and now is the penalty. Today, breaking a covenant means legal hassle and/or financial loss. In ancient civilization, the penalty was losing everything, and possibly your life.

God did not simply claim an *ethnos*. He subjected Himself to an eternal covenant with His claimed people-group. The Creator and the creature in His image, a covenant?

This was not done in satan's kingdom, neither with angels nor with people. Their motto is, "what good is power if you don't use it against others?" The very idea of subjecting themselves to a covenant without deceptive fine print was foreign.

Elsewhere in the *Unseen* Series

Scriptures about fallen Lucifer's trick agreements are explored in Book Three, *Nobody Sees This Creation: The Origin of the Devil and His Replacements*.

THE COVENANT TERMS: GOD

Yahweh unilaterally initiated this covenant and spelled out His own terms. There was no negotiation as occurs between people.

First, He would bring about natural blood heirs for Abraham's wealth and name. Second, Yahweh would bring those heirs out of foreign slavery with wealth after judging the nation that enslaved them. Third, He laid out the schedule from Abraham's point of view. Lastly, He would also give them the land of Canaan for their home.

> Then He said to Abram: "Know certainly that your
> descendants will be strangers in a land that is not
> theirs, and will serve them, and they will afflict
> them four hundred years. And also the nation
> whom they serve I will judge; afterward they shall
> come out with great possessions. Now as for you,
> you shall go to your fathers in peace; you shall be
> buried at a good old age. But in the fourth gener-
> ation they shall return here, for the iniquity of
> the Amorites is not yet complete." (Genesis
> 15:13–16)

God promised two long-lasting results, still present in today's time.

> To your descendants I have given this land, from the
> river of Egypt to the great river, the River
> Euphrates—the Kenites, the Kenezzites, the
> Kadmonites, the Hittites, the Perizzites, the
> Rephaim, the Amorites, the Canaanites, the
> Girgashites, and the Jebusites. (Genesis 15:18–
> 21)

> As for Me, behold, My covenant is with you, and you
> shall be a father of many nations. No longer shall
> your name be called Abram, but your name shall
> be Abraham; for I have made you a father of
> many nations. I will make you exceedingly fruit-

ful; and I will make nations of you, and kings
shall come from you. (Genesis 17:3-6)

THE COVENANT TERMS: ABRAHAM

In a covenant, both parties had obligations. Abraham was assigned a
commitment: YHWH would be the god of the chosen line, and no
other.

> As for you, you shall keep My covenant, you and
> your descendants after you throughout their
> generations. This is My covenant which you shall
> keep, between Me and you and your descendants
> after you: Every male child among you shall be
> circumcised... My covenant shall be in your flesh
> for an everlasting covenant. And the uncircum-
> cised male child, who is not circumcised in the
> flesh of his foreskin, that person shall be cut off
> from his people; he has broken My covenant.
> (Genesis 17:9–10, 13–14)

The Hebrew words translated *made a covenant* include the idea
of cutting. Thus you may hear someone describe it as cutting a
covenant.

Abraham would establish a generational loyalty to Yahweh alone,
symbolized by a physical cutting of each male child before any
personal choice was possible. The foreskins of every male baby's
penis would be removed with a knife on the eighth day. We know it
as circumcision, a unique identifier in ancient society (unlike today).

The men among God's people bore the marks that distinguished
them as His claim. To enforce the generational loyalty, a threat hung
over every new father. If he did not circumcise his sons in loyalty to
the Abrahamic covenant, his own sons would be excluded from the
entire people-group.

Abraham's side of the agreement carried the same penalty as Cain's: exiled, wandering, with the identity of a wanderer who belongs nowhere and is welcomed by no one.

ANCIENT COVENANT

People cemented covenants with ceremonies. The ancient world had two types, parity and suzerainty.

Parity covenants occurred between equals. An exchange of equally valuable goods in security signified the covenant. Abraham had a parity agreement with Abimelech, a nearby king (Genesis 21:27–32).

Suzerainty covenants occurred between a greater person or power (the suzerain) and a lesser. The greater magnanimously granted protection and privilege to the lesser, who would pay tribute and conform to its laws. Kings and Chronicles show several suzerainty treaties made (and broken) by Israel and Judah.

If the lesser failed, the penalty was death or demolition. There was no penalty for the suzerain.

THE LESSER

Consider the circumstances when Genesis 15 opens. Abram is a childless old man, wandering in a foreign land, with no evidence of what God had promised. He had believed Yahweh and received the righteousness reviewed earlier, but he had no visible surety. He asked God for certainty about the future God described would occur.

God caused the concern by choosing the language of inheritance in 15:7. The justifiable expectation of a long-childless man with no heir would be multi-generational.

> Then He said to him, "I am the LORD, who brought
>   you out of Ur of the Chaldeans, to give you this
>   land to inherit it."

GOD PLEDGES HIS LIFE

Yahweh answered Abraham's question about surety with a covenant ceremony which seems strange to us, but well-recognized in Abraham's time.

> So He said to him, "Bring Me a three-year-old heifer,
>   a three-year-old female goat, a three-year-old ram,
>   a turtledove, and a young pigeon." Then he
>   brought all these to Him and cut them in two,
>   down the middle, and placed each piece opposite
>   the other; but he did not cut the birds in two....
>   And it came to pass, when the sun went down
>   and it was dark, that behold, there appeared a
>   smoking oven and a burning torch that passed
>   between those pieces. (Genesis 15:9–10, 17)

Abraham and Yahweh cut a covenant. Included in cutting, symbolized by the division of the animals, was death for failure to perform. The divided animals signified God's submission to the same fate, if He should fail His covenant obligations.

When the fiery object hovered and passed between the pieces, Yahweh saying, "May I be cut in two if I fail My commitment under this covenant." God was upending the usual suzerainty covenant. The greater was pledging His life.

IOU VERSUS COVENANT

The covenant-cutting defines God to the heavenly host. There is no record of a covenant with angels. Scripture never records their understanding of His love, which was a mystery to them (1 Peter 1:12).

In the IOU leverage-based system of satan, the only question is whether you are performing your obligation satisfactorily. Even that standard can change at satan's whim.

In contrast stands the God of covenant. Lucifer could not defeat and replace Him, but understood what His covenant ceremony meant. Imagine satan's shock to witness it: the Spirit most able to impose IOUs instead subjects Himself to obligations with people made of dust.

The topsy-turvy terms of His covenant with Abraham was a first in history for both seen and unseen. This covenant-cut love manifested fully beginning in a Bethlehem stable. God became man, and thirty-three years later bore our covenant failure as if it was His own. God would subject Himself to killing by men.

In satan's IOU economy, there is no loyalty, endurance, or love. Character and integrity are of no matter. But in God's covenant, those qualities are baked in. Righteous character, integrity, and love are essential in His covenant.

Throughout the *Unseen* Series

The trading system of darkness has become increasingly important with each Scriptural exploration. For discerning satan's schemes, it may be the single most valuable discovery in the series: *lest Satan should take advantage of us; for we are not ignorant of his devices.* (2 Corinthians 2:11)

RUBBING IT IN

The enemies next heard God further defining His worldwide blessing through Abraham. The setting in Genesis 18:17–19 makes it particularly dramatic. Abraham's nephew Lot had chosen a heavily-watered region around Sodom to settle his family and herds, leaving Abraham the arid side of the mountains.

One day, three "men" came to Abraham's tent. They had physical bodies, ate, spoke, and appeared capable of normal human interaction. One was Jesus in His physical body, outside time. His two angelic companions travelled to Sodom to inspect and verify its evil while He remained with Abraham, speaking in Sarah's hearing.

Imagine the scene: the pre-incarnate God the Son stands with Abraham at the tent, talking. Abraham is completely unaware at first. God reveals it for Abraham's physical ears, and for the unseen ears of darkness.

> And the LORD said, "Shall I hide from Abraham
> what I am doing, since Abraham shall surely
> become a great and mighty nation, and all the
> nations of the earth shall be blessed in him? For I
> have known him, in order that he may command
> his children and his household after him, that
> they keep the way of the LORD, to do right-
> eousness and justice." (Genesis 18:17–19)

Darkness already knew God planned to bless all nations through Abraham, but they didn't know any specifics. YHWH divulges one blessing in His soliloquy: righteousness and justice for all nations through Abraham's line.

Despite the efforts of darkness, people of every *ethnos* would have access to God and His justice. What's dreadfully terrible for the principalities is miraculous for you and me. What began with God's claim on Abraham would continue through Israel's national existence, and then the Jewish community. The last link in the chain of blessing was a Jewish son named Jesus.

> Now to Abraham and his Seed were the promises
> made. He does not say, "And to seeds," as of
> many, but as of one, "And to your Seed," who is
> Christ. (Galatians 3:16)

CHAPTER 14

GOD'S PEOPLE-GROUP GROWS

THE DEVIL'S WAR TO REPLACE GOD WAS FAR FROM OVER IN his thinking. But now, God had credited spiritual righteousness to a human being. That man would become God's claimed people-group. Through Abraham, their own nations would be blessed.

As eager as darkness was to fight, God had already doomed their hostility. I AM WHO I AM had claimed an *ethnos* of His own. The devil's resistance would be an exercise in futility—like his rebellion in heaven.

HOLY SEPARATE

The Bible word *holy* means apart and separate. In the New Testament, the plural word *saints* translates the Greek ἁγίοις (transliterated *hagiois*, from the root *hagia*), which means to separate.

The principalities only needed to install one sin throughout their claimed society. It was fine for the claimed nations be like one another.

In contrast, God's claim on Israel refused such a low standard. The Law imposed a high positive standard; His people had to be holy, apart, separate. Their agreement with YHWH would distinguish them from other nations, forever.

This is for Us

Maybe you identify holiness by behavior rules, or language rules. What you consider holy behavior may well be symptomatic of holiness.

But biblical holiness means separate. It originates with our inclusion among God's people. We are separate because He is, and we are His.

For I am the LORD your God. You shall therefore consecrate yourselves, and you shall be holy; for I am holy. (Leviticus 11:44)

As He who called you is holy, you also be holy in all your conduct, because it is written, "Be holy, for I am holy." (1 Peter 1:15–16)

COVENANT AGREEMENT

Agreement is the fabric of everything God has made. The nature of the Trinity is multi-personal unity, and it is imprinted everywhere from atoms to galaxies. It's one reason the Bible revolves around God's covenants with people.

But since we are dead in spirit, we don't even know we've entered covenants with God's unseen enemies. The world, the flesh, and the kingdom of darkness dominate human agreements. Like the people of Babel, most people are technically godless because God is a non-factor in their world.

Even religious people sidestep the battlefront and insert God as one agreement among others. It's a way to hedge our bets with a self-serving, self-defined "righteousness" without having to be distinctly holy as people owned by Him.

To be holy and separate strikes at the core of all our agreements.

Whether it's society-wide sins, or our religious behaviors, or our self-image, every agreement comes under His knife when you are a true, growing Christian.

Jesus insists on Lordship. He must be the primary agreement. On Judgment Day, He will sort out entire nations, family lines, and individual people on that basis. The people of Israel will come under harsher judgment because each one of them has an exclusive opportunity to agree with His claim on them and be loyal to Yahweh.

HOLY YOU

Now He offers Himself as Father to you because you yield to Jesus, the seed of Abraham who blesses all nations. Your faith in Jesus grafts you into that covenant agreement. He becomes the Lord of Lords to you, the suzerain you obey and rely upon.

The very night before He died, Jesus said that we become separated out from everyone else. But will we obey? Our answer is very serious for everyone who calls themselves Christian.

> If you were of the world, the world would love its
> own. Yet because you are not of the world, but I
> chose you out of the world, therefore the world
> hates you. (John 15:19)

God's Fatherhood offer is worldwide, to every language and tribe, but not uncontested. The competitors in the nation-claiming arena are clutching onto their claim. Jesus warned that most people would remain in thrall to darkness.

We enjoy oneness with each other in the Body of Christ, so we easily expect similar unity with the unsaved. In fact, the trend is quite the opposite. Whether they know it, people agree with darkness. Right before them, in us, stands the righteousness of God through Christ. They view God as a threat, and He lives in us, so we are the threat they push against.

> He who was born according to the flesh then perse-
> cuted him who was born according to the Spirit.
> (Galatians 4:29)

The process of separation is constant for us. The unseen world is a combat of group-claimers. Righteous followers of the Savior and Lord are arising in every people-group globally. His new covenant is plucking people from territories ruled by very hostile principalities.

ONLY ISAAC OUT OF SIX

God separated one from Abraham's eight sons Scripture names. The six born to him by Keturah and the firstborn Ishmael from Hagar did not inherit the covenant. Isaac, born second, was the child of promise.

> Abraham said to God, "Oh, that Ishmael might live
> before You!"
> Then God said: "No, Sarah your wife shall bear you a
> son, and you shall call his name Isaac; I will estab-
> lish My covenant with him for an everlasting
> covenant, and with his descendants after him.
> And as for Ishmael, I have heard you. Behold, I
> have blessed him, and will make him fruitful, and
> will multiply him exceedingly. He shall beget
> twelve princes, and I will make him a great
> nation. But My covenant I will establish with
> Isaac, whom Sarah shall bear to you at this set
> time next year." (Genesis 17:18–21)

CREATOR OF ALL, FATHER OF SOME

The power of God's promise is demonstrated in the line separated out. Likewise, by walking with Jesus, Christians distinctly manifest the power of His promises. We stand out among the many who forsake those promises today.

Throughout the Bible, God separates people and family lines on an exclusive basis—a stark contrast to the current emphasis on inclusion.

The popularity of the social gospel in the early twentieth century spread a false belief that God is the father of all mankind. He is not. The Bible is clear: He is the Creator of all people, yes. But He is Father only to Jesus Christ and His brothers in faith, both men and women.

WHY NOT FATHER TO ALL

God's plan is to bless people in all the *ethnos*. But our sin is a barrier. His wrath against our race is justified. Every person stands condemned; He is not Father to all people, but Judge. Our offense against our Creator doesn't set the severity, which varies among people. The One offended is Himself the measurement.

That's why we are *by nature children of wrath* (Ephesians 2:3). Only people should satisfy God's wrath; we are the ones who caused the alienation. But it leaves us totally without hope, because we can't make the infinite restitution or restore what God Almighty was deprived by our agreements with darkness.

That's where the Second Person of the Trinity enters the picture. Only God Himself could propitiate the wrath of God. Such a savior had to be fully man and fully God, because only man *should* pay but only God *could* pay. That's why Jesus so confidently stated the exclusivity of access to the Father.

I am the way, the truth, and the life. No one comes to
the Father except through Me. (John 14:6)

Simply because of human generational reproduction, the incarnate Savior had to be born into one family line.

155

SEPARATION METHODS

Why did God single out the younger son to inherit Abraham's covenant? Clearly He wanted Sarah as the mother, but why her? I see several plausible reasons. One might be greater legitimacy for Isaac by their marriage status.

But whatever His reasons, His plan required that the child of promise should defy every natural norm. Indeed, Isaac did—born to a 100-year-old man by his aged, infertile wife who carried Isaac full term.

YHWH would not use that pattern again until the birth of John the Baptist.

ONLY JACOB OUT OF TWO

It's God's habit to separate His claim from everyone else, and it continued with the next generation. Isaac and Rebecca had twins, Esau and Jacob. God attached His claim to the line of Jacob, not Esau.

Separating His chosen while excluding others is God's way. The choosing of some signifies that many are not chosen, and even excluded. Objecting that it is unfair shows that we ignore what is fair to Him. But this separating bore fruit for all time. It ultimately led to our Savior, who had to come from some unique family line.

If God's choice was entirely based on bloodline, most of us would be excluded. But His separating choices has great value to individual people. It means we can be chosen as well.

In Romans 9:6–13, Apostle Paul says the basis is promise, not blood. He uses four Old Testament citations in proving that was always God's way: Genesis 21:12, 18:10, 25:23 and Malachi 1:2–3.

> But it is not that the word of God has taken no effect.
>> For they are not all Israel who are of Israel, nor
>> are they all children because they are the seed of

Abraham; but, "In Isaac your seed shall be called." That is, those who are the children of the flesh, these are not the children of God; but the children of the promise are counted as the seed. For this is the word of promise: "At this time I will come and Sarah shall have a son."

And not only this, but when Rebecca also had conceived by one man, even by our father Isaac (for the children not yet being born, nor having done any good or evil, that the purpose of God according to election might stand, not of works but of Him who calls), it was said to her, "The older shall serve the younger." As it is written, "Jacob I have loved, but Esau I have hated."

The kingdom founded by Esau was Edom; it was long hostile to Israel and the line of Jacob until its judgment and disappearance (Jeremiah 49). Both nations were wiped out by the Babylonians under Nebuchadnezzar, but only the line of Jacob was brought back afterward. Esau's line vanished.

INCLUSION BEGINS

In the next generation of Abraham's line, a marked change occurs. The lineage of promise includes all twelve of Jacob's sons. He is the first patriarch whose sons were all included.

Compare it to the genealogy in Genesis 5. Each man named *had other sons and daughters.* Abraham himself had seven children not chosen, and Isaac had one son not chosen. But not Jacob; God changed his name to Israel, the name which all twelve sons inherited. Together they received the identity as God's chosen people-group.

Through Joseph's compelling life events, God brought all twelve sons into Egypt. He reassured Jacob that their migration to Egypt was His plan (Genesis 46:3–4). Thus began the four hundred years

He had revealed to Abraham, who was long dead when Jacob went into Egypt.

Being God's chosen for the lineage of promise was not a panacea that would offset hardships. God used the word *bless*. We might define that as *easy*, but He did not. He forewarned Abraham about the affliction in store for his descendants.

Elsewhere in the *Unseen* Series

Book Six is *Nobody Sees This Israel: God's Vanguard Against Darkness*. It explores the many ways the Law at Sinai separated the Israelites from all other nations.

FORMATION THROUGH HARDSHIP

Israel's sons would become the nation aligned with God's claim. But it was not overnight; a slow development of national character was required. God had previewed some details about the process ahead for Abraham's line.

> Know certainly that your descendants will be
>> strangers in a land that is not theirs, and will serve
>> them, and they will afflict them four hundred
>> years. And also the nation whom they serve I will
>> judge; afterward they shall come out with great
>> possessions. Now as for you, you shall go to your
>> fathers in peace; you shall be buried at a good old
>> age. But in the fourth generation they shall
>> return here, for the iniquity of the Amorites is
>> not yet complete. (Genesis 15:13–16)

The Savior's line was through Jacob's son Judah, then through David. God's dealings with His people-group from Abraham to Jesus are the bulk of our Old Testament. The Savior of mankind had to come from that one family line. He would inherit the lineage of promise on behalf of all us.

THE CHURCH FOR ALL PEOPLE, AGAINST ALL DARKNESS

Now the time of limitation to one genetic line is past. The invitation is now open to all people, every family, and every *ethnos*. We can be adopted into the family of God.

Apostle Paul describes Jesus as *the first-born of many brothers* (Romans 8:29). Thanks to the advent and work of Jesus, God can be Father to anyone worldwide. You and I can now be included—no matter what group we come from.

> For you are all sons of God through faith in Christ
>   Jesus. For as many of you as were baptized into
>   Christ have put on Christ. There is neither Jew
>   nor Greek, there is neither slave nor free, there is
>   neither male nor female; for you are all one in
>   Christ Jesus. And if you are Christ's, then you
>   are Abraham's seed, and heirs according to the
>   promise. (Galatians 3:26–29)

God's response to the principalities of darkness was choosing Israel. In the free-for-all after Babel, God was claiming one as well.

Israel remains precious to God. But the Church is His Body. We are not an *ethnos,* but God's authoritative force. God created the lineage of promise, all the while intending to create us. His plan has always been to bless all the families of the Earth through Abraham's seed.

We are not a claimed people-group; instead we supersede the *ethnos*. Christians from every nation, cultures, and languages are pushing darkness into retreat.

Jesus' exclamation after Peter's confession signifies this escalation into a force. God never made such a statement to anyone in Israel. In the eyes of the Lord, His church is a force on Earth.

> And I also say to you that you are Peter, and on this
> rock I will build My church, and the gates of
> Hades shall not prevail against it. And I will give
> you the keys of the kingdom of heaven, and
> whatever you bind on earth will be bound in
> heaven, and whatever you loose on earth will be
> loosed in heaven. (Matthew 16:18–19)

> And from the days of John the Baptist until now the
> kingdom of heaven suffers violence, and the
> violent take it by force. (Matthew 11:12)

GOD COMPETES

The dark principalities and rulers were claiming the people-groups formed at Babel, but they were not alone. Yahweh also entered the fray as a competitor. He initiated a covenant with His chosen man Abraham, and subjected Himself to its obligations and penalties. Imagine the shock wave through the kingdom of darkness. How would they react?

CHAPTER 15

AN UNSEEN RULER SUFFERS

THE FALLEN LUCIFER DECEIVED OUR FIRST PARENTS, whose spirits died instantly (Genesis 2:17). With three subsequent strategies over 1,556 years, the opportunistic, power-mad devil leveraged humanity's agreement into a death sentence. The holy God's own image-creatures became odious to Him, and He wiped out all but eight with the Flood (Genesis 6:1-8).

And now God had chosen one nation out of many. Imagine the shock of darkness when God claimed His own nation. If satan had our common sense, he would see that he can't win and resign. But the crazed archangel still saw a way to win. No wonder God said the wisdom of the fallen Lucifer was corrupted (Ezekiel 28:17).

For simple self-preservation, we would seek God's favor by being kind to His chosen people. But satan could only see the odds in his favor. God had one nation; satan's kingdom claimed every other one. The enemies drew a different conclusion when God claimed one group: one ripe, juicy target. That's exactly what He wanted them to conclude.

HENCHMAN MOBILITY

The devil's IOU and reward pattern manifested with Kings Saul, Nebuchadnezzar, and Belshazzar. They offered half their kingdoms and other rewards to others. Imagine the dragon of darkness barking orders and offering rewards to his obligated partners. "Make that nation odious to God, and all humanity will be ours. Whoever achieves that will never be demoted in my kingdom."

God's *ethnos* was not only a single objective for satan. The fallen angels could get out of satan's prison. The devil told Jesus he could give the nations to anyone, but the fallen angels knew it from the outset. Once God had a claim, each principality could prove their value to their overlord, managing empires satan had assigned them to attack God's people-group. The iron-fisted devil promoted and demoted his partners based on performance.

Elsewhere in the *Unseen* Series

Book Three studied the Bible's revelation of satan's prison for the spirits of darkness. Isaiah 14 and the book of Daniel taught Jesus to see the Luke 11 division in their kingdom.

The first henchman with an opportunity to prove itself was the principality over Egypt.

SEPARATION THROUGH GEOGRAPHY

When Pharaoh exalted Joseph to save Egypt from starvation, he also granted the land of Goshen to Joseph's brothers. On the eastern side of the Egyptian delta, Goshen was apart from the main body of Egypt. The many channels of the spreading Nile River came between them. Moses recorded the reason for this selection: Egyptians detested herders of livestock (Genesis 46:34).

Separation is a theme, as we have seen. Yahweh's covenant with Abraham was His carve-out from all the *ethnos*. God promised the future homeland as the geographic form of separation. Whether in Goshen or Canaan, God geographically separated His chosen *ethnos* from the nations claimed by satan's kingdom.

HOLY MEANS SEPARATE

Their long oppression in Egypt also fit God's separating habit. Slavery kept the twelve tribes apart from Egyptians in four ways. Israel remained a unique population through marital, genetic, geographic, and linguistic isolation. Their unique identity as an *ethnos* was safe from the Egyptian principality.

First, none of the Egyptians wanted to intermarry with slaves or shepherds. Second, without intermarrying, His claimed nation descended genetically from Jacob's loins. Third, their specific work restricted them to Goshen. Not only was it separating, but also handy. Living in one geographic territory, close to the Red Sea, God could retrieve them quickly in one night. In Goshen, they remained in a ready state for extraction at the proper time.

Fourth, the Hebrew language developed. They spoke Egyptian, but like many slave populations have done, they developed their own language as a means of privacy. It also gained its written form, used by Moses to record the Law.

GOD'S SUPERIORITY OVER DARKNESS

The powers of darkness have never stopped trying to unseat God. All the events of the Exodus occur in the competitive arena of spirits claiming nations. There, the Exodus has one message: Yahweh is the only God. The showdown with Israel in Egypt repeatedly demonstrates: I AM is superior.

The first demonstration was long beforehand. God was not

surprised that a hostile principality would oppress his descendants. He declared it Himself in the covenant ceremony with Abraham.

The second sign of superiority was Moses himself. Pharaoh decreed infanticide to kill all the generation of Moses. Not only did he survive, Moses was raised as the son of Pharaoh's daughter. Outsmarting the unseen Egyptian ruler, right before the puppet-master, God raised up a deliverer for His own *ethnos*.

What a stabbing wound to satan's pride, to realize Israel's deliverer was in Pharaoh's household all along. Kill the child Moses; no Exodus—if only he had known. It wouldn't be the last time God raised up a deliverer right under satan's nose. The devil would have that stabbing wound again, centuries later in the work of Jesus.

> But we speak the wisdom of God in a mystery, the
> hidden wisdom which God ordained before the
> ages for our glory, which none of the rulers of
> this age knew; for had they known, they would
> not have crucified the Lord of glory. (1
> Corinthians 2:7–8)

Once Moses and Aaron initiated the contest in the natural, God demonstrated His total sovereignty over Egypt's Pharaoh. I AM WHO I AM would repeatedly harden the heart of the vaunted ruler oppressing the Hebrews—the third evidence of God's preeminence.

PLAGUE BACKGROUND

Ancient peoples organized their lives by their divinities. Requirements and promises were a constant preoccupation. As far as that goes, Israel's relationship with YHWH mimicked that universal impulse.

But the principalities were leveraging people into iniquity with IOUs and blackmail. For daily life in each area, a person would need the ruling spirit's help. The entire society relied on their unseen divinity for good harvests and safety from marauders. Pleasing the demigod through sacrifices and honoring behaviors how help was assured—in the pagan mind.

Using the IOU blackmail system, the unseen rulers supposed their rights to be exclusive. When the book of Exodus opens, the people claimed by God had become the slaves of Egypt and their ruler. What could go wrong for Egypt?

COMBAT BY PLAGUE

Plenty. Each time Pharaoh refused Moses, God released a plague that uniquely humiliated the dark rulers from satan's kingdom. The ten plagues are a fourth evidence of Yahweh's supremacy.

Thanks to children's catechisms and Sunday School, the plagues are uppermost in centuries of Bible memory. But there is a reason for what God did with them. Each plague had a rationale based on the identities of Egyptian deities.

Over centuries, the divinities insinuated their corruption into Egyptian society. The day before Moses walked in, the unseen rulers were trusted for favor and feared for requirements. Suddenly, their evil pride was humiliated, outsmarted, and plundered.

The plagues were God's beat-down for each one of Egypt's unseen rulers. He targeted them one by one, and the rights they each had claimed over Egyptian life, shown in the following chart.

Aggravating the humiliation, God distinguished between Egypt and His people. Plagues four through ten affected only Egypt proper. The land of Yahweh's *ethnos* in Goshen received none, not even the thick darkness.

> No one could see anyone else or move about for three
>   days. Yet all the Israelites had light in the places
>   where they lived. (Exodus 10:23)

Egyptian Divinity	Depicted Feature	Humiliating Plague
Hapi	water bearer	water into blood
Heket	head of a frog	frogs
Geb	dust of the earth	dust into lice
Khepri	head of a fly	flies
Hathor	head of a cow	disease on livestock
Isis	goddess of medicine	boils and sores
Nut	goddess of sky	hail
Seth	god of storms	locusts
Ra	sun god	total darkness
Pharaoh	ultimate authority	all firstborn slain

Yahweh had not sent armies, but an old shepherd. The God of Moses had looked quite powerless, vulnerable, even laughable. But with each plague, the unseen rulers learned: His weakness had been a feint before His ambush.

SORCERY MANHANDLED

Each specific plague humbled them distinctly, but that's not all. A fifth evidence of God's sovereignty is the interplay between Moses and the sorcerers of Pharaoh. The unseen rulers had insinuated their magicians into Egyptian government. Now in humble Moses, Yahweh was insinuating His representative among them.

The magicians duplicated the first two plagues; magic arts are real and dangerous. Previously, we reverse-engineered to the schools and the standards for service in Pharaoh's court. The best and most ambitious could rise to the top and serve in the halls of power.

Now as then, God and His people are superior. The sorcerers could duplicate frogs, but could not make them go away. That, only Moses could do. After the third plague, the sorcerers admitted their defeat (Exodus 8:19) and were no longer participants.

WHY THE LONG SLAVERY

A Bible reader has to ask the obvious questions. Why would God let His people suffer under four hundred years of slavery? What divine purpose could cruelty, hunger and premature death serve?

God's Word reveals three reasons for Israel's four-century slavery. First is the time required to make it a just battle in the unseen. In His covenant terms for Himself, God sovereignly declared that it would happen, and announced that the principalities of satan would have a four-century head start.

> But in the fourth generation they shall return here,
>   for the iniquity of the Amorites is not yet
>   complete. (Genesis 15:18)

The Amorites is a summary name for all the "ites" who lived in Canaan. Their unseen principalities had claimed them. God's four-century delay would permit the dark blackmailers to integrate sin fully with their claimed *ethnos*. No one would have an excuse when Israel obeyed God's *herem* command to kill every living soul.

The head start would find the enemies looking back over the shoulders. The enslaving masters of Yahweh's people would witness the multiplication of Abraham's descendants—a second reason for the four hundred years.

> Now there arose a new king over Egypt, who did not
>   know Joseph. And he said to his people, "Look,

> the people of the children of Israel are more and
> mightier than we.... But the more they afflicted
> them, the more they multiplied and grew. And
> they were in dread of the children of Israel.
> (Exodus 1:8–9, 13)

They came as seventy people under Jacob and Joseph. Their multiplication was not a threat to Egypt until the four hundred years neared their end. Being oppressed as slaves did not diminish their love lives but enhanced them.

More populous than the Egyptians themselves, well over a million Hebrews would eventually leave. It explains Pharaoh's alarmed decision to oppress Israel. Nonetheless, overwhelming multiplication continued.

In Pharaoh's mind, that justified what the unseen spirit wanted. To exterminate God's claimed nation, Pharaoh decreed the final solution: kill all the male babies. That would stop the multiplication.

The LORD later states a third reason for the four century wait: its lasting effect on His people. The long slavery they endured made the memory perpetual. They could both respect Him fearfully and confidently enjoy His love and loyalty.

> ...that you may tell in the hearing of your son and your
> son's son the mighty things I have done in Egypt,
> and My signs which I have done among them, that
> you may know that I am the LORD. (Exodus 10:2)

> You have seen what I did to the Egyptians, and how I
> bore you on eagles' wings and brought you to
> Myself. (19:4)

These clearly stated objectives are good. But couldn't they happen more quickly? Why couldn't God Almighty accomplish them with less pain for His people? Because the people were not the focus. It was a competition in the unseen. God's design was maximum justice and pain—for His enemies.

THE INACTIVITY OF GOD A FEINT

What had Yahweh done since entering the competitive arena? After claiming a people-group for Himself, did He contest the unseen enemies' influence?

Elsewhere in the *Unseen* Series

Chapter Six of the *Unseen* Series' second book is titled *Coder and Code, Decoder and Key*. God uses cryptography to hide things from satan, and the code key is a quality that can never be duplicated by the proud devil: meekness.

Warcraft includes subterfuge, coded communications, feints, and ambushes. Scripture repeatedly reveals how God uses such maneuvers with darkness. God has an ambush habit, often including a feint which is a pretense of failure and weakness. The devil is never prepared because God's Word is a coded communication to the meek, which satan can never be.

Israel's battle at Ai in Joshua 8 is one example. Joshua and his first army pretended weakness and retreated at the slightest challenge. The enemy saw Israel's feigned inadequacy, and poured out of their city for a simple mop-up operation.

Suddenly, their city was undefended, and Joshua's second army overtook it. The defenders of Ai had no escape and were defeated between the two armies.

The rulers of the unseen darkness saw no benefit to delay or feint, and could imagine no benefit for God to use it. In darkness, power is *pedal to the metal*. Egypt's unseen rulers would see a competitor in name only.

For four centuries, YHWH offered no actual competition on behalf of His *ethnos* Israel—but this was God's feint.

PRIDE'S FALSE JOYS

Imagine the nightclub scene in the heavenly realms as the powers mocked God's plan. "Hey, those descendants of Abraham—look at them now. We own them! We've got Midian, Edom, Sheba, Dedan, Aram, Kedar, Teman, Amalek! Even that nation God chose, Israel, is defenseless against us!"

How these evil unseen rulers would have savored this apparent victory! In fact, it was Yahweh giving them a long head start.

The flaws in the plan of darkness were unbeknownst to them but not to God. Pride blinded them, and they used power against people. These habits would make them think that God gave up. After all, they didn't see Him lifting a finger to rescue His chosen people from the domination of nations and their principalities.

What a contrast these rulers would have seen between their total defeat in the Flood, and the evident success of their nation-claiming strategy!

"Satan, sir, this is our best strategy yet!"

ENSLAVEMENT A FEINT

The slavery in Egypt is another example of God's feint and ambush. The descendants' long enslavement told the unseen rulers that Yahweh was weak, unable to do anything for His people. Long-enduring disengagement is how the people would see it.

But with this feigned inability, Yahweh was setting up an ambush on some of satan's henchmen. At the right time, He would spring His ambush on Egypt's principality, with the plagues and the Exodus. Then on Sinai would come the very public and eternal consolidation of His own nation, the Jews, from the line of the patriarchs.

It was God's hidden mystery, unannounced and unknown to the principality of Egypt. His ambush with the plagues would shock and confuse the dark enemies.

In the unseen realm, the four centuries were required. A successful unseen ambush would end Israel's long enslavement by Egypt's principality. God was using combat tactics.

DARKNESS RULED THE OPPRESSOR

The enemy satan perceived God and His people-group as powerless, which was exactly the perception intended. The kingdom of darkness set up shop in Egypt, using the hierarchy that Apostle Paul listed in Ephesians 6:12.

A principality propped up Pharaoh, promoting his delusion that he was divine. The subordinate rulers, posing as divinities, claimed influence over multiplying areas of Egyptian daily life: water-carrying, river life, agriculture, religion, and the like. The table above correlated the divinity and its "expertise." Evil forces of wickedness permeated the school of sorcery and its advanced degrees available to the advisors of Pharaoh.

But unbeknownst to them, all the dark rulers were doomed by Yahweh's feint. The ambush was about to be sprung.

COVENANT REMEMBERED AND DOUBTED

When we accept God is wrestling unseen enemies, the plagues and the exodus reveal the hidden mysteries behind the gospel.

Scripture records no divine activity for the vast bulk of four centuries. By the time of Moses' generation, their God was a dim memory. If they remembered God's covenant with Abraham, it may have felt like a fairy tale. We now know the silence of God was purposeful, God's feint versus satan's kingdom.

God was sending Moses back to the Hebrews after a forty-year absence. Moses knew the skepticism and doubt that would greet him. God knew it also and provided him with the signs of his staff, snake, and hand.

But Yahweh's powerful affirmations gave Moses a strengthening resource for the challenge ahead. When God first calls Moses from the burning bush, it's plain He has not given up. He affirms them as "My people" and expresses His care.

> And the LORD said: "I have surely seen the oppression of My people who are in Egypt, and have heard their cry because of their taskmasters, for I know their sorrows. (Exodus 3:7)

A second resource given to Moses was God's own name, considered at length previously.

> Then Moses said to God, "Indeed, when I come to the children of Israel and say to them, 'The God of your fathers has sent me to you,' and they say to me, 'What is His name?' what shall I say to them?"
> And God said to Moses, "I AM WHO I AM." [YHWH] And He said, "Thus you shall say to the children of Israel, 'I AM [YHWH] has sent me to you.'" (Exodus 3:13–14)

Moses' third resource was God's reaffirmation of His covenant with Abraham.

> And God spoke to Moses and said to him: "I am the LORD. I appeared to Abraham, to Isaac, and to Jacob, as God Almighty, but by My name LORD [YHWH] I was not known to them. I have also

> established My covenant with them, to give them
> the land of Canaan, the land of their pilgrimage,
> in which they were strangers. And I have also
> heard the groaning of the children of Israel
> whom the Egyptians keep in bondage, and I have
> remembered My covenant. (Exodus 6:2–5)

The heavily oppressed Hebrews could not receive this news with faith however; the mental footprint of enslavement was far too deep.

> I will bring you into the land which I swore to give to
> Abraham, Isaac, and Jacob; and I will give it to
> you as a heritage: I am the LORD.'" So Moses
> spoke thus to the children of Israel; but they did
> not heed Moses, because of anguish of spirit and
> cruel bondage. (Exodus 6:8–9)

GOD'S NAME ON THE LINE

Throughout the Law, God keeps saying, *I am the LORD.* Why does He do this? He is not egotistical and full of Himself. Quite the contrary: it asserts His loyalty to the four-hundred-year-old covenant. As to Abraham in the Genesis 15 covenant-cutting, God's own identity and name was the surety for Israel's future.

But the dark principalities used blackmail and bribes for their chokepoints. They didn't enter covenants. They had ensnared Egypt with their IOU system for sacrifices, both well-meaning and wicked. The religious practices of Egyptians were all the slaves would see. Sinai's sacrificial guidance was free of IOUs, but lay in the future, unknown to the hapless slaves.

Like their masters, the slaves would think in terms of worship IOUs. To get, you give. But what could these slaves offer the long-ago god of Jacob? They had nothing. Not even faith was possible after their cruel oppression, destitute and despairing as they were. They could enter no divine IOU with their ancient god. He certainly had not acted in any powerful way for them, either. In such a situation, people excuse themselves from even trying.

When the long-exiled Moses returned to the Hebrews after Sinai, they were relieved for a time. The feeling was short-lived when the first plague caused them to work so much harder and suffer so much worse.

> Then, as they came out from Pharaoh, they met
>> Moses and Aaron who stood there to meet them.
>> And they said to them, "Let the LORD look on
>> you and judge, because you have made us abhor-
>> rent in the sight of Pharaoh and in the sight of his
>> servants, to put a sword in their hand to kill us."
> (Exodus 5:20–21)

Maybe they had forgotten the covenant, but God had not. His name was the surety, as the God who had cut the covenant with Abraham.

Moses penned this record looking back. But in the moment, the Hebrews did not know YHWH had pre-planned this slow development of their national character. They didn't remember the covenant ceremony prophecy He expressed to Abraham. The centuries in slavery were not without purpose.

The time of extracting them arrived. What we know as the Exodus was a first in heaven's revealed history: God and man partnered in direct combat with principalities of satan.

The first to suffer: Egypt. YHWH sent Moses to Pharaoh—but not for persuasive diplomacy. Instead, His plan was confrontation, and He described the *how* to Moses:

> But I will harden his [Pharaoh's] heart, so that he will
>> not let the people go. (Exodus 4:21)

Backfire

Repeatedly in Scripture, God lets unseen enemies think certain people are their agents when in fact, His purposes are being served. The chief example is Judas Iscariot (John 17:12). Before him was Cyrus, supposedly set up by darkness' ruler behind Persia, but actually raised up by God & announced 160 years previously (Isaiah 45:1). Before Cyrus was Nebuchadnezzar, who after seven years' insanity finally acknowledged the Lord God as the real ruler, in Daniel 4:35.

> *All the inhabitants of the earth are reputed as nothing;*
> *He does according to His will in the army of heaven*
> *And among the inhabitants of the earth.*
> *No one can restrain His hand*
> *Or say to Him, "What have You done?*

And before Nebuchadnezzar was the Pharaoh.

PHARAOH CHOSE PRIDE

Some have questioned God's fairness in hardening a man's heart into enemy status. But the Scripture clearly says that Pharaoh freely cooperated with the hardening process (Exodus 8:32). We also know the magicians and sorcerers in the king's inner circle—secret implants of darkness—readily supported Pharaoh's hardening.

The I AM WHO I AM reveals His foreknowledge that the Egyptian ruler would choose pride, goaded by his unseen puppet-masters. Just as God turns our sin and tragedy to His purposes, Pharaoh's pride-choice was given an integral role in the plan. God prophesied this to Moses.

> But I am sure that the king of Egypt will not let you
> go, no, not even by a mighty hand. So I will

> stretch out My hand and strike Egypt with all My
> wonders which I will do in its midst; and after
> that he will let you go. (Exodus 4:19–20)

Egypt's susceptibility to the pride of darkness was also developed over generations.

DYNASTY PRIDE

Like all ancients, the Pharaoh who defied Moses' God believed he would meet his ancestors after death. The ostentatious wealth and servants entombed with the Pharaohs bear witness to this belief. Whereas we dread going to hell, Pharaoh's dread would be his ancestors' eternal taunts: "he's the idiot who lost the slaves." Unless he resisted the petition of Moses, he faced eternal shame for diminishing the family pride in the next life.

Such dynasty identity grows over several generations. The principality would amplify the pride with each generation. The Egyptian dynasty pride was well-served by oppressing the Israelites.

By the time of Moses' Pharaoh, fear of ancestors' humiliation outweighed their fear of I AM. Pharaoh's repeated hardening suggests that he feared his ancestors more than the gods themselves.

PRIDE BLINDS WITH FALSITY

The Pharaohs—and the principality who upheld them—had a false sense of security. Their success in oppressing God's chosen *ethnos* blinded them to reality. It wasn't darkness who installed Pharaoh as their representative and regent. It was the LORD.

> But indeed for this purpose I have raised you up, that
> I may show My power in you, and that My name
> may be declared in all the earth. (Exodus 9:16)

God oversaw the Pharaoh's birth. He who holds all things together by His word (Hebrews 1:3) held together the personality, pride and family identity of Moses' Pharaoh. Sovereign over all, Yahweh had permitted the Pharaonic line to develop their hardening pride.

The devil and his cohorts did not see reality then, and they don't now. God always wins. He purposely contrives the timing in His warfare with their puppets. God has even scheduled our maturity as Christians and His Church for the day of our full participation.

Darkness could only consider Pharaoh their man because they fell prey to their own blinding pride. They thought to permanently oppress the nation God chose. That the Hebrews were the feint of a divine Spirit was inconceivable to unseen rulers.

Their plan was a false one. Their Pharaoh had been Yahweh's pawn, not theirs.

REFUSAL TO REPENT

Pharaoh tries to negotiate with God. "Take your men only," only to endure God's subsequent plague of locusts. All crops and vegetation were destroyed (10:10-15).

He next attempts to permit the people, but not the livestock (10:24). His last attempt to dictate terms for God is no more successful. The final plague follows it; Pharaoh's firstborn is killed, with all those of Egypt.

During the drumbeat of disasters, Pharaoh perceives God's supremacy over the gods of Egypt. When he honors Yahweh, he breaks ranks with his dark puppet-master.

> Then Pharaoh called for Moses and Aaron in haste,
>   and said, "I have sinned against the LORD your
>   God and against you. Now therefore, please
>   forgive my sin only this once, and entreat the

LORD your God, that He may take away from
me this death only." (Exodus 10:16–17)

Pharaoh confessed rightly, but didn't repent, as Nebuchadnezzar
would later do. The dynasty pride was bred into him thanks to his
unseen puppet-master. Once the pressure of each plague was
relieved, Pharaoh repeatedly chose pride over repentance. Let us be
warned as well.

Their End Cometh

How remarkably this foreshadows the final judgment of
every opponent at the end of time, in Philippians 2:9-11, when
the rule will be "no take-backs."

Therefore God exalted him to the highest place
and gave him the name that is above every name,
that at the name of Jesus every knee should bow,
in heaven and on earth and under the earth,
and every tongue acknowledge that Jesus Christ is Lord,
to the glory of God the Father.

THE BEST FEINT

Our question remains unanswered. What did four centuries' slavery
achieve that couldn't be achieved otherwise?

It was a feint that required the four centuries in the making, and
included three concurrent operations.

First, God isolated Israel for purity, language, multiplication, and
quick retrieval.

Second, Egypt could develop the false security and dynasty pride
nurtured by its unseen rulers. God desired a showdown in the spirit
world which required the puppet-master's fully matured pride. The

dynasty pride of Egypt would be at a fever pitch and dramatic in its fall.

Third, the people of Canaan would fully earn their judgment by God during Israel's conquest.

These are only justified by God's competitive intention: to ambush darkness dramatically and publicly. The humiliation of darkness would occur as Yahweh beat down the unseen rulers, both where Israel left and where Israel was to go.

THE SHOWDOWN PRODUCES FAITH

Some within Egypt's courts yielded to God's power before the plagues ended. They saw the defeat long before Pharaoh, who would not listen to them. Exodus 8:20 tells of Egyptian officials who feared and respect God's word. When Moses announced the plague of hail, they brought their livestock into shelter.

Imagine the financial reward they would reap, when theirs was the only living livestock in all of Egypt. The breeding fees alone would have far outweighed their value on the hoof.

THE LAST DROP

Unassisted by darkness, Pharaoh might have listened to those advisors who accepted YWH's supremacy. Unhardened human pride would have relented.

That is not the way of darkness. The devil is a destroyer and spared no human expense. For satan's war, Egypt's land was completely destroyed, its agricultural power vanquished, and the carcasses of its livestock rotted in open fields. Wailing for dead children filled the air.

But for the principality over Egypt, that was not humiliating enough. Blindly expecting to win, the evil ruler kept waging war with God, just as it had done in the heavenly realms with Lucifer (Revelation 12:7-8).

Lucifer can only use others and never loves them and likewise, his wicked ruling partners in the heavenly realms. The principality of Egypt was hell-bent on challenging God down to the last drop of blood—that is, Egyptian blood.

And in His frequent habit of judgment, I AM THAT I AM let them have what they wanted: the all-out war at the Red Sea.

ONE MORE FEINT

Yahweh toyed with His enemy. The place names are specific, like using the directions on our phones. In one last feint, He was leading the Hebrews in a purposely circuitous route. God wanted His people to look lost and disoriented to Pharaoh.

> Now the LORD spoke to Moses, saying: "Speak to the
> children of Israel, that they turn and camp before
> Pi Hahiroth, between Migdol and the sea, oppo-
> site Baal Zephon; you shall camp before it by the
> sea. For Pharaoh will say of the children of Israel,
> 'They are bewildered by the land; the wilderness
> has closed them in.' Then I will harden Pharaoh's
> heart, so that he will pursue them; and I will gain
> honor over Pharaoh and over all his army, that the
> Egyptians may know that I am the LORD." And
> they did so. (Exodus 14:1–4)

Knowing Egypt's unseen rulers well, God pressed every advantage. He repeated a feint of weakness and drew Pharaoh's army to the seashore.

The Egyptians and their bloodthirsty principalities interpreted the Hebrews' wandering as a sign of the LORD's weakness. Looking lost signaled the enemy's opportunity to defeat Yahweh's prime objective.

As Seen Today

Their conclusion was half-true, like so many statements of the world. True—the slaves didn't know how to get out of Egypt. True—the slaves were cornered. False—After all those plagues, God still hung them out to dry at the mercy of Pharaoh's army.

That's the patten of Satan's deception: statements which are true in fact but false in their implication. Those facts almost always insinuate that God is only out for Himself and is not reliable to care for us.

Eve bought it. Will we?

The many trade routes of the ancient world offered much easier pathways from Egypt to Canaan, with no impassable bodies of water. Egypt's unseen ruler and his partner Pharaoh conclude, "they don't know how to get out of Egypt, and they're cornered!"

The Red Sea crossing only occurred by God's sovereign will. He had maneuvered them there on purpose. He wanted them cornered there on purpose.

Now the unseen enemy has been lured into God's trap by His appearance of weakness. That's exactly what He wanted the unseen enemies to think, drawing them to press every perceived advantage. That's how a feint works.

Yahweh's goal was to dramatically and publicly humiliate the fallen angels of darkness. It not only justified the long slavery and the plagues. They were also humiliated when Israel crossed and Egypt's army was drowned.

WATER, WATER, WATER

What was God going to do with the opposing rulers? We've previously identified how the evil principalities were associated with cooling water. YHWH brings Israel out of Egypt *through water*.

> Then Moses stretched out his hand over the sea;
> and the LORD caused the sea to go back by a
> strong east wind all that night, and made the sea
> into dry land, and the waters were divided. So
> the children of Israel went into the midst of the
> sea on the dry ground, and the waters were a
> wall to them on their right hand and on their
> left. And the Egyptians pursued and went after
> them into the midst of the sea, all Pharaoh's
> horses, his chariots, and his horsemen. (Exodus
> 14:21–23)

The selection of such a sea-crossing is not accidental. On Day Three, God had raised dry land and displace the moisture-cravers of darkness. In the Flood and division of continents, God teased satan with a water-covered Earth, and again displaced it with dry land. Now comes a third time. God's people take priority; dry land is opened for them in the midst of the sea.

> For the horses of Pharaoh went with his chariots and
> his horsemen into the sea, and the LORD
> brought back the waters of the sea upon them.
> But the children of Israel went on dry land in the
> midst of the sea. (Exodus 15:19)

Water was central in the unseen combat with Egypt. Infant Moses was rescued from the River. The plagues had occurred at the River, the water had produced endless frogs, and frozen water had fallen as hail. Finally Pharaoh is stripped of his army in the Red Sea through which he lost the slaves.

There is a clear message: God was contesting the moisture-craving principality of Egypt. And the newly rescued Israelites clearly perceived it, as their song revealed.

> I will sing to the LORD,
> For He has triumphed gloriously!
> The horse and its rider
> He has thrown into the sea!....
> Pharaoh's chariots and his army He has cast into
>   the sea;
> His chosen captains also are drowned in the Red Sea.
> The depths have covered them;
> They sank to the bottom like a stone...
> And with the blast of Your nostrils
> The waters were gathered together;
> The floods stood upright like a heap;
> The depths congealed in the heart of the sea....
> You blew with Your wind,
> The sea covered them;
> They sank like lead in the mighty waters. (Exodus
>   15:1, 4, 5, 8, 10)

GOD VICTIMIZES A PRINCIPALITY

However strong and long the dark hierarchy held sway over Egypt, their stability ended when the crusty shepherds of I AM walked into Pharaoh's throne room.

> Afterward Moses and Aaron went in and told
>   Pharaoh, "Thus says the LORD God of Israel:
>   'Let My people go, that they may hold a feast to
>   Me in the wilderness.'" And Pharaoh said, "Who
>   is the LORD, that I should obey His voice to let
>   Israel go? I do not know the LORD, nor will I let
>   Israel go." (Exodus 5:1–2)

Pharaoh had no more heard of YHWH than had Moses and the oppressed Hebrews. But the unseen ruler of Pharaoh would certainly take notice. Never in the Bible record had the God of one nation contested against another. Yet that's just what YHWH was now doing on behalf of His claim.

The unseen forces of wickedness thought their domination of Israel was safe. The weak Yahweh could not contest their grip, or so they thought. But they had another think coming. If satan took pride in capturing God's chosen family for four hundred years, he now discovered: it had only been by God's permission.

Israel's deliverance from Egypt provides many evidences proving that He rules, He alone, and there is no other. It's on that basis He claims their loyalty at Sinai.

I, the LORD, am the first;
And with the last I am He. (Isaiah 41:4)

WEALTH PLUNDERED

God also promised Abraham that *afterward they shall come out with great possessions* (Genesis 15:14). With pity (and relief) for the freed slaves, the rank-and-file Egyptians freely offered their wealth to the Israelites. Israel departed, enriched for its journey by the freely offered plunder of Egypt as Yahweh had foretold to Moses.

I will give this people favor in the sight of the Egyptians; and it shall be, when you go, that you shall
not go empty-handed. But every woman shall ask
of her neighbor, namely, of her who dwells near
her house, articles of silver, articles of gold, and
clothing; and you shall put them on your sons
and on your daughters. So you shall plunder the
Egyptians. (Exodus 3:21–22)

His judgment against the nations claimed by darkness often includes plundering by God's people. Jeremiah's prophecy about Babylon's fall is another example.

> "Though Babylon were to mount up to heaven,
> And though she were to fortify the height of her
>   strength,
> Yet from Me plunderers would come to her," says the
>   Lord. (Jeremiah 51:53)

The Hebrews took in a giant haul. It later enabled an entire calf of molten gold, and after that, the tabernacle with its rich fabrics, gold and silver leaf, and solid cast objects.

PRESTIGE TAKEN

Pharaoh stubbornly insisted that his alone was the power to rule Egypt. The principality secretly corrupting the nation incited him and was humiliated by God's power.

The human ruler on the throne also had a share of the humiliation. Pharaoh's honor and prestige was transferred to Moses, a shepherd from nowhere. Pharaoh's own close associates sided with Moses over their superior.

> He who feared the word of the Lord among the
>   servants of Pharaoh made his servants and his
>   livestock flee to the houses. (Exodus 9:20)

> Then Pharaoh's servants said to him, "How long
>   shall this man be a snare to us? Let the men go,
>   that they may serve the Lord their God. Do you
>   not yet know that Egypt is destroyed?" (Exodus
>   10:7)

The man Moses was very great in the land of Egypt,
in the sight of Pharaoh's servants and in the sight
of the people. (Exodus 11:3)

Jesus's parable about the dinner party well describes the humiliation that Pharaoh suffered.

When you are invited by anyone to a wedding feast,
do not sit down in the best place, lest one more
honorable than you be invited by him; and he
who invited you and him come and say to you,
'Give place to this man,' and then you begin with
shame to take the lowest place. (Luke 14:8–9)

Apostle Peter put it this way: *God resists the proud but gives grace to the humble.* (1 Peter 5:5)

PEOPLE FREED

The four hundred years of isolation and preparation ended. God did the impossible: He extracted two million impoverished slaves from the mightiest of Earth's empires. Not before or since has such a thing occurred.

In their wake, they left a decimated Egypt: no crops, no livestock, no firstborn sons, no divinities, and no elite chariot army. The age of Egypt's then-principality was ended.

FOUR HUNDRED THIRTY YEARS LATER...

After Israel's exodus from Egypt, they arrived at Mount Sinai. God there instructed Moses to restate His claim upon them as a people.

Thus you shall say to the house of Jacob, and tell the
children of Israel: 'You have seen what I did to

the Egyptians, and how I bore you on eagles'
wings and brought you to Myself. Now therefore, if you will indeed obey My voice and keep
My covenant, then you shall be a special treasure
to Me above all people; for all the earth is Mine.
And you shall be to Me a kingdom of priests and
a holy nation.' These are the words which you
shall speak to the children of Israel. (Exodus
19:3–6)

FOUR HUNDRED SEVENTY YEARS LATER...

A slight rope around its ankle holds the legendary circus elephant in
place. Likewise, the Israelites could not discard the paradigm of slavery, even after being freed. Immediately and repeatedly after their
deliverance, they disdained God's covenant with them.

Their consequence? God prohibited the exodus generation from
entering the land promised to their forefather Abraham. Instead,
they would wander and die in the wilderness for four decades. Only
their children would enter.

To those children, poised afterward to enter the land of promise,
Moses again restated God's claim on their *ethnos*.

For you are a holy people to the LORD your God; the
LORD your God has chosen you to be a people
for Himself, a special treasure above all the
peoples on the face of the earth. The LORD did
not set His love on you nor choose you because
you were more in number than any other people,
for you were the least of all peoples; but because
the LORD loves you, and because He would keep
the oath which He swore to your fathers, the
LORD has brought you out with a mighty hand,
and redeemed you from the house of bondage,

from the hand of Pharaoh king of Egypt.
(Deuteronomy 7:6–8)

THE NATION OF THE I AM

In the Exodus, the people-group of I AM WHO I AM was activated. Israel began interacting with the nations of darkness as a nation themselves. Each people-group represented their gods, and Israel would represent Yahweh among them all.

We think of Mt. Sinai as the place where God gave the Law. With thirty centuries of hindsight, we know this law is the best way to live for all humanity.

However, the participants themselves lacked such hindsight. Every event was new and had a unified purpose: to separate the chosen people of God from the nations claimed by darkness.

Every element of the Law serves that purpose. Yahweh made them His own. The game of the ages was afoot.

CHAPTER 16

THE SHUFFLING OF THE CLAIMERS

THE NEW TESTAMENT WRITERS HAD ONE BIBLE, OUR OLD Testament. Apostle Paul had the most advanced knowledge of it. But many Christians today consider the Old Testament irrelevant or primitive.

For Paul to write about the principalities and rulers of wickedness, there must have been Old Testament support. Jesus was a man of Scripture, and always said it must be fulfilled. There must have been Bible guidance for His deliverance ministry. He was ready when satan came to tempt; our Old Testament warned Him.

How would Jesus and the Bible authors see the wicked principalities in the Old Testament?

THE NATIONS JUDGED BECOME DESERTS

The national prophecies in Ezekiel were my first clue. When God judged them, He dried up the rivers of those lands. But how is desertification a punishment for the nation-claiming principalities?

Jesus revealed the cravings of darkness in Luke 11:24 and 16:24.

Book Three of the *Unseen* Series covers this in depth, with other scriptures. His teaching about the demons' travels and the flames of hell only makes sense under one condition: for evil spirits to have rest, they seek moisture.

As Seen Today

Even today a satellite photo reveals what God did. The lands of the ancient world, where those nations once existed with large cities, are barren desert now, bereft of population— and of water.

Our physical bodies are sixty percent water, and we are the ones they are assigned to oppress. But when God dries up a geography in judgment, people leave them. Without people for moisture, the fallen angels suffer their inward flame anew—the moisture they craved, no longer accessible there.

When Yahweh declared His wrath against an *ethnos,* the rulers of wickedness suffered the wrath as well.

Many *ethnos* nations are judged in the Old Testament. Moab, Ammon, Philistia, Assyria and other principalities receive prophetic judgment. But the volume and content on "the Big 3" of Egypt, Tyre & Babylon is far greater.

THE BIG THREE

Babylon was not a nation like ours, but a city-state. Its empire prospered only under one king, Nebuchadnezzar, and relied on military conquest. From their subjugated vassals, Babylon imported the most qualified into its service and culture, as in Daniel 1:3-4. Babylon collapsed when it suffered military conquest by Cyrus.

Tyre, in contrast, rose to power through economic power and

widespread trading—just as Lucifer had done. He himself was its principality, God reveals in Ezekiel 28. Tyre's extensive trading was identified in detail by God; His prophetic judgment on it was the termination of all trade.

Elsewhere in the *Unseen* Series

The contrasting trade systems of heaven and hell are very significant in God's final judgment. Book Ten of the *Unseen* Series explores them throughly: *Nobody Sees This Victory Yet: The Destruction of Darkness.*

Egypt, the third of "the Big 3," was a true nation. One king and one national agreement united many inhabited cities. Its power and influence always originated with its agricultural fertility. This made Egypt the breadbasket of the ancient world and gave it a non-military international influence. That's why the patriarchs repeatedly fled to Egypt when famine struck Canaan. God's judgment of Egypt consisted largely of judgment on agricultural process, including the waters.

PRINCIPALITY TO HELL

Both Isaiah and Ezekiel received prophecies about God's judgment on Egypt. How could a nation be cast down to hell? The prophecies' words only make sense if the principality is the one whom God judged.

Consequence for enslaving God's people? God's wrath casting it down to hell. Consequence for losing the slaves? satan's fury, returning it to the prison of the Pit.

The devil assigned a different fallen angel to claim Egypt, which had built up its power again. Scripture does not reveal that directly, but by implications. Over seven centuries after the Exodus, the human nation had again become prominent.

WATERLESS PIT PARADIGM

Jesus and the NT authors had the right paradigm to find the Old Testament basis about nations and nation-spirits. The following Scriptures are cryptic, and near impenetrable, without this paradigm.

Yahweh declared judgment on Egypt again. In the prophecy of Ezekiel 31–32 are hidden hints about Jesus' death, the Spirit's pouring out on the many-membered Church, and the partnership of that Church with God's judgment.

> "Thus says the Lord God: 'In the day when it
>   [Egypt] went down to hell, I caused mourning. I
>   covered the deep because of it. I restrained its
>   rivers, and the great waters were held back. I
>   caused Lebanon to mourn for it, and all the trees
>   of the field wilted because of it. I made the
>   nations shake at the sound of its fall, when I cast
>   it down to hell together with those who descend
>   into the Pit; and all the trees of Eden, the choice
>   and best of Lebanon, all that drink water, were
>   comforted in the depths of the earth. They also
>   went down to hell with it, with those slain by the
>   sword; and those who were its strong arm dwelt
>   in its shadows among the nations.
> 'To which of the trees in Eden will you then be
>   likened in glory and greatness? Yet you shall be
>   brought down with the trees of Eden to the
>   depths of the earth; you shall lie in the midst of
>   the uncircumcised, with those slain by the sword.
>   This is Pharaoh and all his multitude,' says the
>   Lord God." (Ezekiel 31:15–32:10)

For God to judge Egypt required its waters to be restrained. This led to its trees wilting. And that was it: Egypt fell, cast *down to hell, to the Pit, the depths of the earth.* Is God speaking about the human kingdom, Egypt? The people in its kingdom are mentioned, but the judgment requires a spirit which only its unseen principalities and rulers had.

SPIRITS CAST DOWN

I believe the one judged is the principality who claimed dominance over Egypt. The phrase, *cast it down,* was first uttered in the time of Genesis 1:1, when only angels existed. Earth was pristine and perfect when Lucifer rebelled. God described the penalty: *I cast you out of the mountain of God... I cast you to the ground.* (Ezekiel 28:16-17)

God cast Egypt *down to hell, together with those who descend into the Pit.* The fate of Lucifer is there also, as Ezekiel was told.

> They shall throw you down into the Pit, and you
>> shall die the death of the slain in the midst of the
>> seas. (Ezekiel 28:8)

JUDGMENT OF DRYNESS

God's words use archetypes from Day Three in Genesis 1. He's revealing more than ordinary trees of Egypt. *The trees of Eden* are prominent, and the widely known forest of ancient Lebanon is another symbol, because neither then existed. They too were cast down to the depths of the earth and to hell with Egypt's principality and its many slain.

God reveals what they have in common: *All that drink water.* The withholding of water and dryness of desiccation appears throughout Scripture as God's judgment. We would not think this way unless we saw what Jesus later taught: there is no water in the kingdom of darkness. They crave moisture to soothe the inward fire of God's eternal wrath.

> When an unclean spirit goes out of a man, he goes
> through dry places, seeking rest. (Luke 11:24)

> Send Lazarus that he may dip the tip of his finger in
> water and cool my tongue; for I am tormented in
> this flame. (Luke 16:24)

God is judging the principality dominating Egypt. Consider these phrases from above.

> I made the nations shake at the sound of its fall....
> They also went down to hell with it, with those
> slain by the sword; and those who were its strong
> arm dwelt in its shadows among the nations.

SHOCK WAVES

Other unseen rulers shuddered at God's judgment on Egypt's principality. Ezekiel's prophecy requires Egypt to be prominent among nations, which shook at its fall and went to hell with it. But in his time, natural Egypt was not; its glory was long past. All Egypt's regional influence was lost in the defeat of Pharaoh Necho and Egypt's armies at Carchemish in 609 BC.

With the unseen paradigm, God was speaking not of the earthly nation but the unseen principality. It enjoyed a prominence in the kingdom of darkness. When God judged the wicked ruler, it stripped the remaining principalities of all confidence, and ultimately cast them down to hell with Egypt's principality.

Lastly, Egypt had someone described as *those who were its strong arm*. Is it their soldiers? Yes, but not necessarily only soldiers. The judgment tells us: these *dwelt in its shadows among the nations*. Those who dwell in the shadows are those of the unseen world, which Paul has identified as *principalities, powers, the rulers of the darkness of this age, spiritual hosts of wickedness in the heavenly places* (Ephesians 6:12).

WHY JUDGE THE WATERS

Ezekiel's revelation shows there is a principality of Egypt, and it is being judged by God. The subsequent portions add the evidence of water. For God to judge this principality requires judgment on its waters.

> And it came to pass in the twelfth year, in the
>   twelfth month, on the first day of the
>   month, that the word of the Lord came to
>   me, saying, "Son of man, take up a lamenta-
>   tion for Pharaoh king of Egypt, and say
>   to him:
> 'You are like a young lion among the nations,
> And you are like a monster in the seas,
> Bursting forth in your rivers,
> Troubling the waters with your feet,
> And fouling their rivers. (Ezekiel 32:1–2)

Water features in both the identity and judgment of Egypt's principality. God likens it to Leviathan, as *a monster in the seas*. Its recognizable handiwork was the ruination of water.

It had not been us who crawled out of the primordial soup, but satan. He ventured onto dry land when there were only two people to deceive and seduce. Likewise now, his partners must find moist locations to deceive the nations. Only in this way can they satisfy their moisture craving.

Judging them means judging their waters. This unlocks several mysteries in Old Testament prophecies.

THE JUDGMENT INSTRUMENT

God declares not only the judgment pending then, but the one pending today as well.

> Thus says the Lord God:
> "I will therefore spread My net over you with a
>   company of many people,
> And they will draw you up in My net." (Ezekiel 32:3)

Ezekiel's prophecy describes the work of this company as simple net fishing. The principalities ruling Egypt had been dominant on Earth for centuries. Yet a simple net, spread by God, ensnares it.

Principalities are helpless against God's net, the company of those filled with the Spirit of God. Psalm 149 affirms that we Christians are this *company of many people*.

> Let the saints be joyful in glory;
> Let them sing aloud on their beds.
> Let the high praises of God be in their mouth,
> And a two-edged sword in their hand,
> To execute vengeance on the nations,
> And punishments on the peoples;
> To bind their kings with chains,
> And their nobles with fetters of iron;
> To execute on them the written judgment—
> This honor have all His saints. (Psalm 149:5-9)

The active ingredient in God's judgment of principalities is the Church. Now you know two place in the Old Testament—Psalm 149 and Ezekiel 32:3—where Jesus saw His famous declaration about hell.

> On this rock I will build My church, and the gates of
> Hades shall not prevail against it. (Matthew
> 16:18)

The work of the new people of God, the saints, is to *execute vengeance on the nations*. Exactly what written judgment are we executing on them? The judgment written in Ezekiel, Isaiah, and the other prophetic writings of the Old Testament.

Many such OT verses are better explained when we understand the unseen realm, and in particular, the nation-claiming strategy of satan's kingdom.

Elsewhere in the *Unseen* Series

As we shall see in Book Seven, *Nobody Sees This Warrior: God's Secret Ambush*, God ultimately disarms the enemies' nation-claiming. All available bottlenecks are threatened when anyone can be filled with His Spirit. This passage hints at the widespread multitude that will result: *a company of many people.*

In the above, God has forewarned the principality of Egypt and all the kingdom of darkness that a great company of people will be instrumental in their destruction. He has used no code to promise that it will happen; its certain occurrence is plainly understandable to them.

But with His code, God did hide the who, when and how. These are elements of the outcome that the kingdom of darkness cannot begin to guess. No principality would see any threat in the weak, the meek, and the poor in spirit.

DESERTIFICATION

No code key is needed to learn the exact punishment for Egypt's unseen principality.

> Then I will leave you on the land;
> I will cast you out on the open fields,
> And cause to settle on you all the birds of the
>   heavens.
> And with you I will fill the beasts of the whole earth.
> I will lay your flesh on the mountains,
> And fill the valleys with your carcass.
> I will also water the land with the flow of your blood,
> Even to the mountains;
> And the riverbeds will be full of you. (Ezekiel 32:4–
>   6)

DISCOVERIES SUMMARIZED

Let's highlight how darkness rules the many through the few. We have found unseen realities, hidden in the Bible.

- The fallen angels, cast down to Earth, became satan's principalities and rulers when their rebellion failed in heaven.
- They each craved moisture to offset *the fire in their midst.*
- Humanity's division at Babel enabled them to rule the many through the few.
- Principalities claimed the *ethnos* groups assigned to them by the fallen Lucifer, now satan.
- Geographical places weren't enough. The presence of water and people was required.
- The unseen rulers ensnare the group's leaders using a

bribe/blackmail system of IOU trades, often including the real power of sorcery.

- The leaders then serve darkness as chokepoints and bottlenecks, and lead their *ethnos* in sin, to cause God's holy wrath against them.
- The devil rotates his unseen henchmen, explaining the rise and fall of nations. The success of people-groups ebbs and flows as a result.
- Their ambition is to make God hate His image-creature and destroy it, returning dominion over Earth to satan and his kingdom.
- God permitted all this. He's the one who made it possible by dividing us at Babel. The language-groups gave rise to people-groups with unique governments, cultures, and religions.
- God called one man and cut a covenant with His image-creature. From that man, He claimed a nation for Himself and named it Israel.
- Through Israel's centuries of trials and blessings, God revealed the unseen rulers for the New Testament writers and the Church today to understand.
- From Israel, He brought forth a Savior for all people, to be filled with His Spirit.
- As He promised to Abram: *in you all the families of the earth shall be blessed*.
- With I AM WHO I AM living in us, we occupy the NOW with Him.
- We will execute His judgments upon the principalities.

That's why we wrestle them.

For we do not wrestle against flesh and blood, but
against principalities, against powers, against the

rulers of the darkness of this age, against spiritual hosts of wickedness in the heavenly places. (Ephesians 6:12)

CHAPTER 17

NOT AGAINST FLESH AND BLOOD

WHAT GOOD IS ALL THIS UNDERSTANDING? WHAT benefits do you get? For closed-minded individualists, these discoveries hold limited benefit.

But that's your old life. Now you really can wrestle spirits.

In this book and throughout the *Unseen* Series, people are making Bible discoveries they've heard nowhere else. Such paradigm re-orientation is not instant.

NOT WHO BUT HOW

As of this writing, change long desired by many is breaking out in America, and impacting the halls of influence in Western civilization. You may wonder why I didn't name names of leaders and countries today.

My direction from God is to equip you for the discernment He wants you to have, rather than tell you what and who I discern. None of His Bible prophets or apostles or even Jesus led movements to upend the natural world. You walk with God. Then you will see and do what He had in mind.

Then I will raise up for Myself a faithful priest *who* shall do according to what *is* in My heart and in My mind. (1 Samuel 2:35)

BE A DISCIPLE

Do not feel lost, but persist in yielding yourself to Jesus.

If anyone desires to come after Me, let him deny himself, and take up his cross daily, and follow Me. For whoever desires to save his life will lose it, but whoever loses his life for My sake will save it. (Luke 9:23–24)

His requirement is all, not some. He will help you in ways that seem strange. First, He will help you die to your fragile self. In Exodus 4, He threatened to kill Moses then and there, but for most of us it's little by little.

Through the process, your life will be both lost and saved, and He will activate you in the right way at the right time. The salvation He means isn't merely going to heaven at death. The eternal life is NOW.

SNAPSHOT OF EXISTENCE

The New Testament's Greek word for nations is *ethnos* (not to be confused with our modern political entities). The entire Bible reveals that God is the supreme manager of all Earth's nations. Also revealed: the *ethnos* nations are the battle front of His kingdom and satan's.

The entire spirit world interfaces with our language groups, ethnic cultures, geographic territories, and national governments (all implied in *ethnos*). This is true of the satanic hierarchy, but also true of God and the holy angels loyal to Him. And the heavenly competition for nations is age-old, not limited to our time.

This is humbling for proud humanity, for us and our ethnic groups to be chess pieces on a heavenly board. But considering how our race turned its back on our Creator, this is our just desserts. Made in His image, we distrust Him and persistently believe His enemy. He must judge rebellion.

The Bible reveals God is not only Judge but also Lover. The love of God is our refuge. Yahweh claimed one people-group for Himself, and through them He has willingly provided the entire world a Savior.

Now individuals within every people-group can love Him. Rather than reject us forever, He seeks our salvation through repentance and obedient faith to the Man He anointed, Jesus, as Lord and Savior. Hundreds of millions from every *ethnos* have accepted the undeserved offer.

He habitually separates His own from the nations of darkness and forms us into His chosen people. Now Earth's nations are the battleground, and we are His army. The visible world manifests satan's war against God, but the Church is not limited to the visible.

UNDERSTAND CHURCH HISTORY

In the Church's two-thousand-year history, our perception of the unseen *ethnos* has been a pendulum swing, both in Scripture and in life.

From the Church's founding to the fall of Rome, the writing church fathers exemplified the place of individuals in the worldwide gospel penetration. But when Rome collapsed, the calamity in all economic, social, and governmental systems pushed the pendulum to an extreme. There was no system for satisfying individual desires. Power was possible only for large groups and institutions.

From that point until the Reformation of 1517, the individual virtually disappeared. Only those well-connected to the broad machine of the Roman church could entertain individual aspirations, from bishops to the feudal lords to the Popes and kings. All others need only comply with King and Church.

When the gospel of salvation by faith was restored, the individual sprang to life. Here was a decision available to every human being. Doctrinal divisions and polity conflicts identified the bloody wars that ensued, but more fundamental was the entire view of human existence. Do individuals matter, or only King and Mother Church?

Balance did not result; the pendulum went to the other extreme. The individual became all that mattered. Whether Renaissance or Enlightenment, whether revolutions or revivals, the power of King and Church became subordinate to individual curiosities, beliefs, and ambitions. The frontier expansion of America and its international victories promoted a can-do attitude that has produced the well-known American individualism.

Now at the opening of the 21st century, we are at the farthest extreme of individualism. In most public presentations, the gospel, knowing God, churches, answered prayer, and other Kingdom privileges are only for individuals.

If we do mention any *ethnos* people-groups, it's to blame them for racism and its injustice. Ethnic identification is disdained for all but the aggrieved.

But as Christians and the Church mature, we understand that the unseen principalities are contesting God for humanity nation by nation. We are rising to play our part.

UNDERSTAND YOUR PLACE

We know what's next: the pendulum must return to a resting state of plumb. As individuals combined into Christ's Body, we can function effectively in the war of nations. We can be God's net over principalities, a great company of people executing the judgments written. That is we were saved into.

We each make an individual contribution in the heaven-wide contest. But in America it's easy to be a navel-gazing Christian. Look at your prayer list, your Bible notes, your sermons. What significance do they give to the combat in the heavens? What place do you give your nation? Your culture and its mountains of influence?

Where God is, is the primary reality. That spirit world is why He saved and activated us. Knowing about the nations' unseen kings unlocks history for us, and we can avoid the extreme swings.

UNDERSTAND GOD'S WORD

How many people consider the Old Testament irrelevant? Many Christians rely on favorite verses from it but have given up hope of understanding it.

Knowing how the unseen kings manipulate people-groups unlocks the entirety of the Old Testament for you. Recognizing that God claimed one *ethnos* for Himself helps you understand His simultaneous love and anger for the disobedient Israel.

In the Bible, you can now recognize all the unseen kings that satan showed Jesus to tempt Him. When the pendulum balance is restored, you truly see both the individuals and the nations in the Bible.

Reading the scriptures for the people-groups will unlock the entire Bible for you. Use the Jeremiah 25 Bible study example to train your eyes to see them in scripture. Once you see them, you can't *not* see them.

LOYALTY BEYOND YOURSELF

All of us experience real flesh and blood opposition. Many Christians find solace in the first half of Ephesians 6:12, *we wrestle not against flesh and blood*. But how can a regular person relate to the second half?

> But [we wrestle] against principalities, against
>   powers, against the rulers of the darkness of this

age, against spiritual hosts of wickedness in the
heavenly places.

Christians can try to avoid spiritual wrestling like that. With
timidity, we can withdraw into the protective turtle shell of our spiritual life. How disappointing it must be to General Jesus when a
Christian loves comfort more and shrinks back. Will He slap us, like
General George Patton famously slapped a frightful soldier?

Focus on our own preservation is disloyalty. Such soldiers are
AWOL, willfully forsaking our call to the combat of heaven. Well-
known defensive sayings describe what we do: shelter in place; duck
and cover; stop, drop, and roll. Revelation 21:8 warned us earlier:
cowardice is lumped in with murder and adultery.

You are appointed to fight in the arenas of the unseen kings.

YOU'RE IN THE ARMY NOW

Our calling is global, and our mission field is the *ethnos* of our world.
We've visited Psalm 149 often. Being God's warriors is a joyful honor
for people who are loyal to Him, and never something to avoid or
shortchange.

> Let the saints be joyful in glory;
> Let them sing aloud on their beds.
> Let the high praises of God be in their mouth,
> And a two-edged sword in their hand,
> To execute vengeance on the nations,
> And punishments on the peoples;
> To bind their kings with chains,
> And their nobles with fetters of iron;
> To execute on them the written judgment—
> This honor have all His saints. (Psalm 149:6–9)

You and I are mission-capable to wrestle against principalities.

Do you feel like it? That question does not matter; the Word of God says you are.

Throughout the *Unseen* Series, I cite Jesus' first teaching in the New Testament. His beatitudes in Matthew 5:1–12 spell out not only the qualities to *be in* His saint army, but also what happens when we are.

> For theirs is the kingdom of heaven.
> For they shall be comforted.
> For they shall inherit the earth.
> For they shall be filled.
> For they shall obtain mercy.
> For they shall see God.
> For they shall be called sons of God.
> For theirs is the kingdom of heaven.
> For great is your reward in heaven.

Those very big consequences are for a *they*, not a *you*. Holing up in your shell is contrary to your citizenship in God's claimed *ethnos*, and reflects poorly on your sincerity on Judgment Day.

UNDERSTAND THE HOLY SPIRIT'S PRAYERS

The unseen world of evil spirits motivates us to pray in tongues because we have a new perspective on its effectiveness.

The early Christians knew the Spirit had filled them by speaking in tongues. Apostle Paul prayed in tongues more than others (1 Corinthians 14:2–19). In group settings, the unique gift of tongues required interpretation. He did not say that speaking in tongues had ended; hundreds of millions of Christians testify it definitely has not.

Paul wrote that when our mouth is speaking in unintelligible tongues, the Holy Spirit is praying. In that setting, interpretation is not expected. In fact, we may not understand what we are praying in tongues.

For we do not know what we should pray for as we
ought, but the Spirit Himself makes intercession
for us with groanings which cannot be uttered.
Now He who searches the hearts knows what the
mind of the Spirit is, because He makes intercession for the saints according to the will of God.
(Romans 8:26–27)

Consider how often we have a phone conversation and do other
things simultaneously. I speak in tongues constantly while thinking,
writing, and working.

The battle front of nations equips us to yield our tongues to
Him. Paul said He intercedes for the saints; he didn't limit it to the
saints *around you.* If you have ever found yourself overtaken in
prayer, burdened to the point of travail, it may be *ethnos*-level engagement you are part of.

Be alert to that possibility. When He is praying with your mouth,
ask Him if it's principalities and rulers He is rebuking. Whatever He
replies, you will relish the joy of being His partner. It is a twenty-
four-hour joy and honor.

Let the saints be joyful in glory;
Let them sing aloud on their beds. (Psalm 149:5)

UNDERSTAND THE ENEMY

How do you know what spirit you might be wrestling? By understanding the hierarchy and the relative assignments of each level in
darkness, you are far better equipped for your own function as a
warring spirit.

It's the devil at the top, and under him, the fallen angel that
claimed your *ethnos.* The lowest caste are demons, released on an as-
needed basis and territorial, periodic, and expansive. When needed
for the principalities' battle strategy, they erect obstacles to retard

Jesus' earthly kingdom-building. He himself warned they could travel in eights, seeking their palliative moisture in people (Luke 11:24–26).

But as Paul wrote in 1 Corinthians 2:8, the devil didn't know Jesus' true intent, to die for sin and release the Holy Spirit on all flesh. A bevy of seven installed themselves in the life of Mary Magdalene, but couldn't keep her once Jesus came. Thus the satanic plan backfired, as usual.

DELIVERANCE FROM DEMONS

In the natural, medical and psychological advancement identifies and cures a growing number of organic problems, which become more visible as a result. I myself have had five heart surgeries, chemotherapy, implants, and protective medicines. We welcome the solutions developed.

Likewise, in the world of spirits, a growing body of church wisdom has made deliverance ministry more accessible than ever. The protocols necessary for effectiveness and protection are now widely proven. We can perceive the expansion of unseen demonic oppression as a result.

As in Jesus' time, swarms of demons oppress individuals, all the more as the end draws near. I seek deliverance ministry whenever a repeated oppressive symptom becomes clear to me. Medical, deliverance—it's both/and. Who wouldn't want that?

It is the lowest caste of satan's kingdom that deliverance expels. Their dark lord assigns them to obstruct and oppress individual people. In proper deliverance, those demonic interlopers are prohibited from oppressing you without your welcome.

PENETRATING PEOPLE-GROUPS

But deliverance is distinct from wrestling with principalities. Such spiritual forces of wickedness work on the *ethnos* level. It may be a language-group, or a mountain of culture, or a political nation's government.

Your recognition of the battle front for nations elevates your outreach effectiveness and that of your church, both locally and worldwide.

Apostle Paul's missionary travels manifest how we can penetrate principalities. We travel more than anyone in history with our modern transport modes. Nor is geographic relocation necessary for Americans, because the world's nations come to us: as international students, immigrants, skilled workers, and tourists. And within our own reach, most churches have ethnic subgroups.

Each of these generational families has characteristic sins, implanted by the ruling forces of wickedness. We may find the sins and the ethnic habits disgusting, as ours may be to other *ethnos*. But to war against principalities requires you and your church to love those in thrall to the sins imposed by their heritage. Making disciples of every nation makes this a necessity.

My wife and I have long experience in multi-cultural outreach, more than enough to know how little we know. This has been our purposeful habit in both paid and volunteer ministry. Penetrating a principality's territory is not meritorious; we do it not for ourselves but for the salvation of souls from every tribe and language. The gospel must be delivered. Aiming at anything less is likely for our own satisfaction.

INTERCEDING FOR NATIONS

We need not touch the ground of the lands we pray for, nor understand their cultures. It's unlikely we will meet many kings or people in authority.

Yet we have the weapon that doesn't require any of that: God's prayers in our mouths. Wrestling against principalities means that we pray for specific nations, to expose, disarm, and expel the unseen rulers and interwoven iniquities.

An excellent resource for targeting principalities and nations is https://operationworld.org/.

Apostle Paul wrote a blank authorization for using our intercessory weapons at the highest level, for peaceful lives and for people's salvation. *Without wrath and doubting* signifies their opposites must characterize our intercession: love and confidence.

> Therefore I exhort first of all that supplications, prayers, intercessions, and giving of thanks be made for all men, for kings and all who are in authority, that we may lead a quiet and peaceable life in all godliness and reverence. For this is good and acceptable in the sight of God our Savior, who desires all men to be saved and to come to the knowledge of the truth. For there is one God and one Mediator between God and men, the Man Christ Jesus, who gave Himself a ransom for all, to be testified in due time, for which I was appointed a preacher and an apostle—I am speaking the truth in Christ and not lying—a teacher of the Gentiles in faith and truth.
> I desire therefore that the men pray everywhere, lifting up holy hands, without wrath and doubting... (1 Timothy 2:1–8)

DISCIPLESHIP, EVANGELISM, MISSIONS

In person-to-person evangelism and disciple-making, as well as church ministry, we must reject stereotypes wrongly applied to everyone in a group as if homogenous. However, ethnic reputation can alert us to unseen influence, in ourselves and those we disciple.

Stereotypes may be justified or not. We use them only to be alert in our lives, as iniquity or sin excused for that ethic identity.

Anyone can have heritage-based sin. When you go to a new doctor, they ask your family health history because many conditions are inherited. The same is true in the unseen.

Each of us has an ethnicity of origin, ruled by a principality, installing habitual sins. Nations are identifiable not merely by their flags and leaders, but by their shared iniquity and inclinations to sin. Individuals may not be affected, yet every *ethnos* is widely known by their common iniquity.

Knowing them tells you the relevant scriptures and specific language to use in your gospel ministry. Jesus offers a specific freedom from a specific inclination to anyone with that heritage. But can He offer through you? Understanding nation-claiming makes it possible.

By seeing the unseen war for nations, you recognize the tendrils of a person's ethnic principality, and bring freedom from a prison cell they never saw, the national identity insinuated by unseen rulers.

Missions is transformed as well. A church can ask God for the principality to target. Elevated from mere missionary support, a church can give money and pray persistently against the unseen ruler of a specific *ethnos*. Words of knowledge and wisdom are equally valuable to isolated missionaries abroad. Engaging the nation-level entity is of great help to missionaries in door-to-door evangelism and one-to-one influence.

REPRESENT THE JUDGE

Engaging unseen rulers must not make you obnoxious. But we are truthful. Call it what it is. The kingdom of darkness has captured the bulk of humanity by nation-claiming.

Every social and human injustice occurs in that context. Human suffering is heart-wrenching. Many people are triggered to fight by the mere presence of injustice; we thank God for them. God said to Moses, *I have heard the cry of My people.*

Whether victim and perpetrator, each person is in the prison of satan. Jesus announced Himself with Isaiah's prophecy about that.

> The Spirit of the Lord God is upon Me,
> Because the LORD has anointed Me
> To preach good tidings to the poor;
> He has sent Me to heal the brokenhearted,
> To proclaim liberty to the captives,
> And the opening of the prison to those who are
>   bound;
> To proclaim the acceptable year of the Lord,
> And the day of vengeance of our God. (Isaiah 61:1–
>   2)

We Christians are how He does it all over Earth. Our advocacy begins in heaven's courts, amid the principalities, where we represent the Judge. God revealed His justice system to the prophets, and Jesus' behavior was governed by it. It's a love-system of conversation, agreement, and expression.

> Thus says the Lord of hosts:
> If you will walk in My ways,
> And if you will keep My command,
> Then you shall also judge My house,
> And likewise have charge of My courts;
> I will give you places to walk
> Among these who stand here. (Zechariah 3:7)

> I can of Myself do nothing. As I hear, I judge; and
>   My judgment is righteous, because I do not seek
>   My own will but the will of the Father who sent
>   Me. (John 5:30)

God is the judge of others on this Earth. As Abraham said to God when Sodom's destruction was the topic, *Shall not the Judge of all the Earth do right?* Our righteousness is God's spiritual impartation, not our platform of superiority. Like Jesus, we listen to Him and represent His situational judgments carefully.

We wrestle not against flesh and blood. Our war against injustice is with His weapons and strength, in ways and times He directs. It starts in the heavenly courts, and that may be where He dispatches you. Others He places in the courts of law, public resolve, or relief for unjust suffering. The Judge you represent will direct you if you talk with Him.

BODY POLITIC

I believe that a principality's only involvement with individuals is bribing chokepoint leaders. Culture influencers are one category, and government officials are another. They, in turn, have an influence on appointees and bureaucrats throughout our body politic. Bribed with power, the compliant puppets weave characteristic sins throughout their *ethnos*.

American democracy uniquely empowers each Christian to exert an opposite, godly influence upon leaders. We seat them or unseat them with our elections.

Elected leaders can be two-faced hypocrites, but we have to elect someone. The constitutional offices of government will be filled. Politicians need our vote. Our vote has a bribing power all its own, for righteousness.

We voters can group our influence, whether in churches or in civic groups or campaign volunteering. The more votes you and I can influence, the more influence we have for righteous government.

We represent Jesus' own political influence. He is not only King of Kings, but also the Senator of senators, the President of presidents, and the Judge of judges.

Discipleship to Him and enlistment in His army requires us to exert our influence and thus oppose principalities at every level of the American body politic.

NOW START

After reading, we have a joyful part to play. It starts with the high praises of God in our mouths.

When Lucifer rebelled in heaven, God didn't fight him. Instead, that task was delegated to Michael. Likewise, a war is afoot here. Nations are the battle-ground. We are God's wrestlers.

CHAPTER 18

BIBLE STUDY EXAMPLE:
JEREMIAH 25

THIS SINGLE CHAPTER AND ITS NOTES SHOWS THE enlarged understanding of the heavenly realms after the paradigm of nations is added to our Bible reading. How much more effective can Christians be in their prayer, evangelism, and church life? We are the partners of God, the saints honored to execute the judgments written (Psalm 149).

25:1 The word that came to Jeremiah concerning all the people of Judah, in the fourth year of Jehoiakim the son of Josiah, king of Judah (which was the first year of Nebuchadnezzar king of Babylon), 2 which Jeremiah the prophet spoke to all the people of

> The O.T. dating system used the kings' length of rule. In our traditional dating this is 605 BC, where BC = *before Christ* and AD = *year of our Lord.* Those who dislike the centrality of Jesus call it *BCE* (before common era) and *CE* (common era).

Judah and to all the inhabitants of Jerusalem, saying: 3 "From the thirteenth year of Josiah the son of Amon, king of Judah, even to this day, this is the twenty-third year in which the word of the LORD has come to me; and I have spoken to you, rising early and speaking, but you have not listened. 4 And the LORD has sent to you all His servants the prophets, rising

> Jeremiah was long faithful; called in 617 BC, it's now 594 BC. Jesus said the least in His kingdom is greater than Jeremiah even (Mt. 11:11).

early and sending them, but you have not listened nor inclined your ear to hear. 5 They said, 'Repent now everyone of his evil way and his evil doings, and dwell in the land that the LORD has given to you and your fathers forever and ever. 6 Do not go after other gods to serve them and

> He was one of many prophets who gave the warning summarized here.

worship them, and do not provoke Me to anger with the works of your hands; and I will not harm you.' 7 Yet you have not listened to Me," says the LORD, "that you

> Their disloyalty and disregard for God's first two commandments caused the Lord's punishment; the other commandments are rarely mentioned.

might provoke Me to anger with the works of your hands to your own hurt.

Nebuchadnezzar is named by Jeremiah thirty-seven times. 27:8 tells why, because God appointed that king as His tool of judgment on the principalities—as the dream of Daniel 4 portrays.

8 "Therefore thus says the LORD of hosts: 'Because you have not heard My words, 9 behold, I will send and take all the families of the north,' says the LORD, 'and Nebuchadnezzar the king of Babylon, My servant, and will bring them against this land, against its inhabitants, and against these nations all around, and will utterly destroy them, and make them an astonishment, a hissing, and perpetual desolations. 10 Moreover I will take from them the voice of mirth and the voice of gladness, the voice of the bridegroom and the voice of the bride, the sound of the millstones and the light of the lamp. 11 And this whole land shall be a desolation and an astonishment, and these nations shall serve the king of Babylon seventy years. 12 'Then it will come to pass, when seventy years are completed, that I will punish the king of Babylon and that nation, the land of the Chaldeans, for their iniquity,' says the LORD; 'and I will make it a perpetual desolation. 13 So I will bring on that land all My words which I have pronounced against it, all that is written in this book, which Jeremiah has prophesied concerning all the nations. 14 (For many nations and great kings shall be served by them also; and I will

Against these nations all around: The time of God's leniency on the unseen kings of darkness is over. They successfully made Israel odious and used God's exclusivity against them by introducing false divinities. Now He will make them desolate deserts, with inhabitants as joyless as they remain today.

Nebuchadnezzar and Babylon had God's call to shuffle the unseen kings and their puppet peoples, yet remain liable for their own principality's insinuated sin. Once desertified, sands buried Babylon from living memory about 600 AD.

repay them according to their deeds and according to the works of their own hands.)' "15 For thus says the LORD God of Israel to me: "Take this wine cup of fury from My hand, and cause all the nations, to whom I send you, to drink it. 16 And they will drink and stagger and go mad because of the sword that I will send among them."

17 Then I took the cup from the LORD's hand, and made all the nations drink, to whom the LORD had sent me:

18 Jerusalem and the cities of Judah, its kings and its princes, to make them a desolation, an astonishment, a hissing, and a curse, as it is this day; 19 Pharaoh king of Egypt, his servants, his princes, and all his people; 20 all the mixed

> Jesus would have read this: when God sent Jeremiah to the unseen kings. When satan showed Him all the kingdoms from a mountain, Jesus would remember this event. Unlike satan, God didn't need a high mountain because time and space are no limits to Him, in contrast to the fallen angels of darkness.

> God punishes the disloyalty of His own *ethnos*, and is also reshuffling the principalities. Having tolerated their competition and the influence of their claimed nation, God's judgment is not only for Israel, but for those who corrupted His claim.

multitude, all the kings of the land of Uz, all the kings of the land of the Philistines (namely, Ashkelon, Gaza, Ekron, and the remnant of Ashdod); 21 Edom, Moab, and the people of Ammon; 22 all the kings of Tyre, all the kings of Sidon, and the kings of the coastlands which are across the sea; 23 Dedan, Tema, Buz, and all who are in the farthest corners; 24 all the kings of Arabia

> Where does God takes Jeremiah—to the human or unseen kings? No matter; He can do both easily. *The coastlands* signifies the undiscovered peoples. Imagine the prophet's wonder at this transport.

and all the kings of the mixed multitude who dwell in the desert; 25 all the kings of Zimri, all the kings of Elam, and all the kings of the Medes; 26 all the kings of the north, far and near, one with another; and all the kingdoms of the world which are on the face of the earth. Also the king of Sheshach shall drink after them.

> The LORD of hosts signifies that all the unseen beings are subject to the lordship of the I AM. *The God of Israel* is a loyalty name about His claimed *ethnos.*

27 "Therefore you shall say to them, 'Thus says the LORD of hosts, the God of Israel: "Drink, be drunk, and vomit! Fall and rise no more, because of the sword which I will send among you." ' 28 And it shall be, if they refuse to take the cup from your hand to drink, then you shall say to them, 'Thus says the LORD of hosts: "You shall certainly drink! 29 For behold, I begin to bring calamity on the city which is called by My name, and should you be utterly

> Jesus prayed about *this cup* the night before He died. Jesus would have read that Jeremiah saw it and made all nations drink it, the cup of the Lord's wrath against rebel spirits and the human sin they implanted into their nations. Imagine yourself reading this, knowing that you would substitute for all people and nations under this heavy judgment. How brave! No wonder Jesus received authority over them all (Mt. 28:18).

> Your *ethnos* and its land is the time-piece, the measure, the provocation for You to withdraw the leniency for satan's partners and their claimed nations. As goes Your Israel, so goes all the nations and their unseen kings. Israel is YOUR bottleneck for blessing the many through few.

unpunished? You shall not be unpunished, for I will call for a sword on all the inhabitants of the earth," says the LORD of hosts.'

30 "Therefore prophesy against them all these words, and say to them:

'The LORD will roar from on high,

> Which Person has a shout and voice? The Second Person, Jesus, the Word of God with a body of earth.

And utter His voice from His holy habitation;

He will roar mightily against His fold.

He will give a shout, as those who tread the grapes,

Against all the inhabitants of the earth.

31 A noise will come to the ends of the earth—

For the LORD has a controversy with the nations;

He will plead His case with all flesh.

He will give those who are wicked to the sword,' says the LORD."

> The I AM uses this language of judicial courts often, because Justice receives unflagging respect in the unseen. He intends for us to press His cases for Him versus the unseen kings (Ps. 149).

32 Thus says the LORD of hosts:

> God warns of the coming reshuffling of the *ethnos* and their unseen claimers, in the sixth through third centuries before Christ.

"Behold, disaster shall go forth

From nation to nation,

And a great whirlwind shall be raised up

From the farthest parts of the earth.

33 And at that day the slain of the LORD shall be from one end of the earth even to the other end of the earth. They shall not be lamented, or gathered, or buried; they shall become refuse on the ground.

> The puppet kings will have no more citizens and mourn the loss of bribes from their unseen puppet masters.

34 "Wail, shepherds, and cry!

Roll about in the ashes,

You leaders of the flock!

For the days of your slaughter and your dispersions are fulfilled;

You shall fall like a precious vessel.

35 And the shepherds will have no way to flee,

Nor the leaders of the flock to escape.

36 A voice of the cry of the shepherds.

And a wailing of the leaders to the flock will be heard.

For the LORD has plundered their pasture,

37 And the peaceful dwellings are cut down

Because of the fierce anger of the LORD.

38 He has left His lair like the lion;

For their land is desolate

Because of the fierceness of the Oppressor,

And because of His fierce anger."

> The unseen rulers may have thought them-selves safe, as if I AM WHO I AM was power-less or uncaring to let them contest His claimed *ethnos*, just as He previously let Israel be enslaved by the prin-cipality of Egypt for four centuries. But that would be wrong. His feint is terminated; His ambush is sprung. I AM will now oppress them with the anger they stored up for them-selves. The tables are turned.

This single chapter and its notes shows the enlarged understanding of the heavenly realms after the paradigm of nations is added to our Bible reading. How much more effective can Christians be in their prayer, evangelism, and church life? We are the partners of God, the saints honored to execute the judgments written (Psalm 149).

223

CHAPTER 19

READER ENGAGEMENT RESOURCES

THE WIDER THE PUBLICITY ABOUT THE *UNSEEN* SERIES and the greater the fruitfulness, the more readers and listeners wants to be part. There are several ways.

BETA READERS

Each chapter has been tested by beta readers. They help sharpen each book of the *Unseen* Series.

My loyal beta readers represent many age groups and walks of life. Unknown to you, each reviewed this Book Four in manuscript form. Such servants earned all our gratitude; they catch many potential misunderstandings and add much clarity to my writing.

If you would like to volunteer as a beta reader for future installments of the *Unseen* Series, please sign up at the Paradigm Lighthouse website.

BOOKSTORES & REVIEWS

Please tell your bookstore what you think of this book. If no bookstore is near, visit online booksellers to purchase and then review *Nobody Sees These Enemies: How to Discern and Disarm Unseen Tempters*. Examples include traditional booksellers such as BarnesAndNoble.com, social media for readers such as Goodreads.com, and online-only stores such as Amazon.com.

You review as a reader helps someone else feel safe to purchase and benefit from this Book Five of the *Unseen* Series. Your review can help release others from spiritual victimization. From your own online shopping, you know the value in the number of reviews—whether or not the reviewer agrees. Short or long, general or specific, like or dislike, your review will make a positive impact.

SOCIAL MEDIA

If the book imparts understanding to you, please help publicize it for others to gain in the same way. Please friend/follow/like/engage with Paradigm Paul Renfroe on your social media. Subscribe to the podcast, *The Unseen Realm with Paul Renfroe and Friends*. Post your picture with the book, and/or include the purchase link to ParadigmLighthouse.com/books-and-products. Our ranking among booksellers benefits when people search for the book by name.

PODCAST GROUP DISCUSSION

I record online Bible studies with friends, and release them as my podcast to help a larger audience engage with Scripture about the unseen realm. Please help the ranking by subscribing to the podcast, titled *The Unseen Realm with Paul Renfroe and Friends*. Posting it in your social media will also help.

A fellowship is growing around the *Unseen* Series, a place we can discuss and test our Bible discoveries about life as spirits, among evil spirits. Each reader can request log-in credentials at ParadigmLighthouse.com.

PREQUEL (FREE)

Our free fifty-two page prequel to the series is titled, *How to Unveil the Unseen and Live as a Spirit.* Visit ParadigmLighthouse.com to get yours free. We can also supply you copies for your small group Bible study and other fellowship groups.

Churches often have study groups for books like this one that help us know and apply the Bible. The appendix of this book includes discussion questions for each chapter and other Reader Engagement Resources.

SUPPORT BIBLE TEACHING

In the dedication you read about the Paradigm Underwriters. These are people whose giving is responsible for the *Unseen* Series of books and podcast.

Your support frees my time to write and publish the remaining books. It also covers the expenses of book production and overhead expense for today's technology.

Please join my wife and me in producing this *Unseen* Series for the benefit of many. We will execute the judgment written on our shared enemies when Christians understand it.

ABOUT PAUL RENFROE

Paul Renfroe is a Memphis native and Florida resident, with his wife Diane Renfroe. They have two sons and one grandson.

Their ministry and publisher is Paradigm Lighthouse, created to implement the mind of Christ in people born as spirits. They are also licensed insurance agents who help people who want to preserve their savings or have their estate plans up to date.

Paul & Diane are ordained for ministry under the leadership of Apostles Tom and Jane Hamon (Vision Church at Christian International, Santa Rosa Beach FL) with advance ministry degrees from the Ministry Training College. In their church journey they have served at every level of leadership except pastor.

Paul's academic endeavors include a Bachelor of Arts with Distinction from Rhodes College (Memphis TN), where he majored in Bible and Church history while minoring in Philosophy. After graduation, he and his wife served twelve years as campus staff and state directors for InterVarsity Christian Fellowship.

He has also served as board chairman for several nonprofits and helped found one school and two churches. Paul's ability to see what others don't has produced several turn-arounds with nonprofits and ministries previously in decline.

Paul's life includes eight fatal diagnoses from doctors since birth with a heart defect. He has received many healings, both with and without doctors. Paul has also participated in healing many people from various ailments from blisters to brain-death.

Paul's vision for the *Unseen* Series developed over five decades of following Jesus sacrificially. His reputation for knowing the Bible is rarely exceeded. With practice he has an acute ear for God's voice, and a sharp discernment of the topics people wrestle with.

In the *Unseen* Series, this depth and breadth has been condensed for you to go higher up and further in. May God bless you as He has Paul—with lifelong hunger for intimacy with Him.